CLIFFORD

Also by Harold R. Johnson

Fiction
The Cast Stone
Corvus
Charlie Muskrat
Back Track
Billy Tinker

Nonfiction
Firewater: How Alcohol Is Killing My People (and Yours)
Two Families: Treaties and Government

CLIFFORD

A MEMOIR

A FICTION

A FANTASY

A THOUGHT EXPERIMENT

HAROLD R. JOHNSON

ANANSI

Copyright © 2018 Harold Johnson

Published in Canada and the USA in 2018 by House of Anansi Press Inc.
www.houseofanansi.com

All rights reserved. No part of this publication may be reproduced or
transmitted in any form or by any means, electronic or mechanical, including
photocopying, recording, or any information storage and retrieval system,
without permission in writing from the publisher.

House of Anansi Press is committed to protecting our natural environment.
As part of our efforts, the interior of this book is printed on paper that
contains 100% post-consumer recycled fibres, is acid-free, and is processed
chlorine-free.

22 21 20 19 18   1 2 3 4 5

Library and Archives Canada Cataloguing in Publication

Johnson, Harold, 1957–, author
Clifford : a memoir, a fiction, a fantasy, a thought experiment /
Harold R. Johnson.

Issued in print and electronic formats.
ISBN 978-1-4870-0410-1 (softcover).—ISBN 978-1-4870-0411-8 (EPUB).—
ISBN 978-1-4870-0412-5 (Kindle)

1. Johnson, Harold, 1957–. 2. Authors, Canadian (English)—21st
century—Biography. 3. Autobiographies. I. Title.

PS8569.O328Z46 2018   C813'.6   C2018-900343-X
C2018-900344-8

Library of Congress Control Number: 2018934053

Book design: Alysia Shewchuk

Canada Council   Conseil des Arts   ONTARIO ARTS COUNCIL
for the Arts   du Canada   CONSEIL DES ARTS DE L'ONTARIO
                                        an Ontario government agency
                                        un organisme du gouvernement de l'Ontario

*We acknowledge for their financial support of our publishing program the Canada
Council for the Arts, the Ontario Arts Council, and the Government of Canada
through the Canada Book Fund.*

Printed and bound in Canada

MIX
Paper from
responsible sources
FSC
www.fsc.org   FSC® C004071

This humble work is dedicated to my older brother Clifford Melton Johnson. His earliest and lifelong ambition was to be a scientist, to think beyond the boundaries of his place of birth, and to explore ideas even larger than his home planet. To Clifford's children, Clifford Jr., Brian, and Daniel: it is my hope to honour your father. And, of course, to my father, Hildor Johnson, and my mother, Mary Elizabeth Johnson, who are equal parts of my story.

"Deep in the human unconscious is a pervasive need for a logical universe that makes sense. But the real universe is always one step beyond logic."

From "The Sayings of Muad'Dib"
by the Princess Irulan

— Frank Herbert, *Dune*

HOME

THE CHAIR STANDS ON THREE LEGS, the fourth broken off and missing. It defies logic, defies gravity. I wonder whether it was *the* chair. Is that the one? It had once been a pale shade of green that was common in the fifties. Now most of the paint is gone and the wood has turned grey with age.

Is that the one he sat in?

I turn away. That isn't the memory I came here to recover. The old house seems determined to continue standing, despite carpenter ants, wood rot, squirrels, mice, and birds. One whole corner of the ceiling sags, mouldy and water stained. Against the odds a single pane of glass remains in the west window; the other three, the victims of slingshots and mischief. The sunlight through the window sparkles on a broken shard before it strikes a floor littered with mouse droppings and squirrel mess. That floor had once been covered with shiny new linoleum.

There are memories here that I want to remember; the linoleum is one of them. It's a gentle memory of not much consequence.

They'd brought the new flooring home, moved all the furniture outside, rolled the linoleum out, and tacked it down around the edges. It covered the trap door that led to the cellar, and we had to wait until it was worn and the imprint of the door showed through so that my father knew where to cut it.

I remember Mom's cellar. The whole floor sags toward the centre of the room, and I don't trust it to carry my weight. If the joists weren't so rotten, it might be interesting to open it up and have a look down there. It won't be much. Just a sandpit and plank shelves. But those shelves — the memory eases back — once held exactly a hundred jars. Canned blueberries, cranberries, strawberries, saskatoon berries, gooseberries, currants, raspberries, canned moose meat, canned fish. Everything she could preserve went into jars and down into that cellar: pickled carrots, green tomato relish, canned beets.

There's something about smells and memory; I'd heard somewhere that the two work together. I am probably smelling only mould, but my memory is of a huge bin of potatoes and sawdust. I remember turnips and cabbages.

I remember the ladder and I remember brothers.

Clifford came running into the house, and the cellar door was open. He fell into the hole, somersaulted, and would have broken his neck when his head went between the rungs if it hadn't been that Richard, standing at the bottom of the ladder, caught him at the last second.

Good memories. This house had once crawled with children and I was one of them. A family of nine raised here. The oldest grown and gone before I arrived. I'm the seventh. There's a six-year gap between Clifford and me. He was born here in this house on the coldest day of the year, December 14, 1951. Three years later another baby died at birth. Mom blamed the midwife. I was born in a hospital.

These interior walls had once been covered in new blue paper, a pale blue, almost sky blue, and the room was bright and the paper absorbed the happiness of the family. I was a child running around here, and there are still atoms that were once in my body that are now in these walls, in this paper, and, I am sure, there are atoms that were once in these walls that are now in me. I am part of this place. And this place is part of me.

Home:

Does it feel that way anymore?

I examine emotions.

What does it feel like to come back here?

I stand still and listen to my heart, try to clear my mind of spinning thoughts and pay attention to the flow and ebb of stirred feelings: a happy child playing contentedly, the grief that returned at the sight of the chair, the hush of a family's voices.

I conclude *no*, it doesn't feel like home anymore; there's too much distance, too much time between here and me. Here I was a child and the world was a different place. Now I am someone else, changed, shaped by my experiences, my successes and my failures, into the person I am today.

Today I am the searcher.

Searching for what?

For memories?

Maybe for a connection.

Connection to what?

To my beginning.

To look back at the path travelled and attempt to conceive it as a coherent line of succession; from there to here, through that and this, shaped by joy and then by grief until I am the man who stands in an old house falling down, with a floor perhaps too rotted to safely stand upon.

Is that rotted floor a metaphor for my life?

I stomp a booted foot against it, drive a heel down hard. It echoes loudly in the empty room, a solid thump. The wood beneath the floor sounds solid, different from the way decayed wood should sound. I take a step forward toward the centre of the room and stomp again, and again I hear only the reverberations of dry, solid wood. The floor is safe to walk upon. The foundation is sound.

From outside, in the sunlight of an early September afternoon, the house in the pines appears tranquil with its sagging roofline and tarpaper shell. The remaining wooden slats nailed to hold the paper in place are grey with age; the paper itself is torn and ragged, and in places where it's completely missing, the plank interior of the wall shows through.

The words *tarpaper shack* stand out in the jumble of thoughts running through my mind with all of the connotations that phrase implies: of poverty, of the fringe of the greater society, of survival, and even of a little shame.

Yes, that's exactly correct.

My roots are in a tarpaper shack.

I feel myself stand up straighter, perhaps from a stiffening spine.

Tarpaper poor.

The paper feels brittle between my fingers and tears easily when I pull against it. A huge swath peels away from the wall and reveals shiplap planking, rich reds and browns in sharp contrast to the other sun-bleached grey boards. Beautifully aged, here is wood a cabinetmaker would give his eye teeth for, the colours and the grain, how the reds flow down the length. Thoughts of a planer and sandpaper and a little oil to bring out the lines: *I could make something nice from these.*

But would I?

More likely just take them home and put them in a pile and not get around to doing anything with them. And could I really tear down my childhood home and turn it into furniture? It doesn't really belong to me; I still have brothers and it's as much theirs as it is mine.

But I can still look. More black paper on the grass, more wood, more grains, more colours.

What the—

It rolls a couple of feet before it falls over onto its side. I just stand here, not believing. I don't believe because it is impossible. The thing doesn't exist. It's something I made up, imagined, wrote down in my memories, a fragment, a figment. It never really happened, a lie I had told myself so often that it began to feel like truth.

I touch it with my foot. It moves. It is there. Despite impossibility, Clifford's hula hoop lies on the ground in front of me.

I reach to pick it up.

Hesitate.

Do I dare?

Of course I could.

It's just a hula hoop, a piece of plastic tubing in a circle with a stub of a handle that Clifford wired in place.

The memories come in a rush:

I

LEO TOLSTOY AND MY DAD

MOM SAID THAT DAD sat on a wooden chair and held on. I go back in. I have to confront that chair. It could be the same one.

Dad:

He would have been eleven years old when his family emigrated from Sweden. He was the oldest of six. Next in line to him was Julius—Uncle Joe. Most of what I know about Sweden and their early life in Canada came from Joe. Joe liked to talk. Dad didn't.

Clifford once told me he overheard a conversation between Dad and Uncle Joe. They had been arguing. Dad was saying that our family were Laplanders. I later learned that *Lapp* or *Laplander* were derogatory terms for the Sami peoples, the reindeer herders, of northern Sweden, Norway, Finland, and Russia. These Indigenous peoples were treated as harshly by the governments in their countries as were Indigenous peoples here. Uncle Joe wasn't agreeing. Clifford said Uncle Joe's final comment was "I am not one of those."

We don't know much about Dad because he didn't talk. My older brother Clarence remembered going to the trapline with him, to a cabin about fifteen miles south along the shore of Montreal Lake: "We'd leave Molanosa walking together, and by the time we got to the lake, Dad would be a half-mile ahead. By the time I got to the cabin, he'd have a fire going and everything put away. There was a man who could walk."

Other stories mingled in; Uncle Ben, my mother's younger brother: "We shared that trapline at Skunk Point, your dad and me. I'd offer him a ride back to town in my truck, but he never would. Preferred to walk."

Clarence again: "We'd be there for three days and he wouldn't say a word. He trapped in one direction and I checked traps in another. When we came back to the cabin at night, he might say something if it was important, like if he saw fresh moose tracks or something; otherwise, not a word."

Mom didn't know much more about him; he never told her. And what he did, couldn't be completely trusted. He said he was born in 1900. His birth certificate said he was born in 1898. He said that was wrong.

Uncle Joe, on the other hand, who had aspirations of living to be over a hundred like his aunt, said that he in fact was born in 1898, and that his birth certificate, which said that he was born in 1900, was wrong. Joe always wanted to be older than he was and Dad wanted to be younger.

"He lied about his age," Mom remembered. "When we met, he said he was thirty; he was really forty. I might not have married him if I had known he was that old. I was only twenty."

Putting it together: Dad was fifty-nine when I was born.

That's too old to be a father. It's not fair to the children; they get shortchanged.

So, he would have been . . . Let's see, he was born in '98, Mom was born in '21 . . . He was twenty-three years older than her.

They met in '41, during the war.

If it hadn't been for Leo Tolstoy, I wouldn't be here.

Images of Tolstoy in Russia — or, rather, images from the Michael Hoffman movie *The Last Station* with Christopher Plummer—interpose themselves with those of the old house. The connection feels real even though it is quite tenuous.

The Doukhobors were called *Spirit Wrestlers* by the Russian Orthodox Church. The church was trying to ridicule them; instead, the Doukhobors took the name for themselves. They were spirit wrestlers. They wrestled with the established church and with the words of the Bible until they found a definition for themselves: pacifists, agriculturalists, vegetarians whose motto was "toil and a peaceful life." In 1885 they refused conscription, burned their guns, and pissed off the tsar. At the time Russia and Britain were skirmishing along the Afghanistan border.

Tolstoy, also a pacifist who influenced Gandhi, helped the Doukhobors immigrate to Canada. When they got here, they set to work building collective farms. Canada, of course, wanted them, wanted immigrants who knew how to farm. There's a letter from the government of Canada to the Doukhobors that promises, among other things, that if they came to Canada, they would never be compelled to take up arms.

All was good, or relatively good.

Then there was the Second World War.

And there was that other group of pacifists, the Mennonites.

Not much different from the Doukhobors, they both lived their religious principles, both groups preferred to live and farm collectively, both refused conscription. But the Mennonites were Germans. And Canada was at war with Germany. And since Canada was making life miserable for the Mennonites, it was only fair to make life miserable for the Doukhobors as well.

Those who refused conscription were given the choice of jail or work camps. Some chose jail; others chose to go to northern Saskatchewan and build a road through the boreal forest as part of the war effort. In the summer of 1941, about seventy Doukhobors were conscripted, constructing what was to become Highway 2. They lived in tents and worked on the road with rakes, shovels, and axes.

My father, and this is where we begin to know something about him, had joined the army like everyone else. However, he didn't end up overseas. He was released from basic training. They had been marching across a wooden bridge and the bridge collapsed. The inside of his leg, from the ankle to his crotch, was ripped open by a spike, and the wound would not heal at the knee. I never saw it. Mom said the scar looked like a piece of clear plastic.

By the time I got into the armed forces in 1975, we were told during basic training that when we marched across wooden bridges, we were to break stride because if we all brought our feet down in unison, the vibrations could cause a bridge to come apart.

We don't know where my father was for the two and a half decades between when he left the family homestead at about the age of fourteen to go work as a farm labourer to when he was released from the military because of his wounds. He came back to Saskatchewan and showed up here in the North as a foreman over the Doukhobors.

His mother died just before he left home. He said his father was incapable of looking after his siblings so he took them to the neighbours'. The 1930s happened. He told a few stories, mere glimpses of his life, of riding the rails, travelling across Canada looking for work: "I saw these people, Indians, they had a big pot and were cooking. I asked if I could get something to eat. They all had their heads down, kinda ashamed, I guess. One of them says to me, 'We're eating gophers.' I said, 'If you can eat it, I can eat it.'"

But other than these few snapshots, there's a big chunk of his life that we cannot account for, that he never spoke of, not because he had something to hide: he just wasn't a man of words.

So, if it hadn't been for Leo Tolstoy's helping the Doukhobors, the Doukhobors' immigrating to Saskatchewan and being forced to work on a highway in the North, and my father's finding a job as their supervisor and meeting my mother, I wouldn't be here.

MOM AND BABY BROTHER STANLEY

THE CHAIR, THE THREE-LEGGED CHAIR, isn't talking either. It stands mute. All I have with me in the house is Clifford's hoop over my shoulder, Mom's stories, and dim memories.

Mom said her father was working with the surveyors, going ahead of the highway construction crew, showing them the way through the forest. Dad met Grandpa at work and came over for tea, and that's how they met.

Now Mom:

Mom's family comes from a totally different direction from Dad's: Indians, Cree Indians, to be precise, Nihiyithaw. They'd been living at Big Trout Lake in 1928, when all that country was turned into Prince

Albert National Park. Mom said, "They came and told us, 'This is a park now, you have to leave,' and we did. Left everything behind, our houses, our gardens, everything."

They moved to the north end of Montreal Lake, near where the adhesion to Treaty 6 was negotiated and signed in 1889.

Where Montreal Lake ends and Montreal River begins, there's a bit of high ground. A natural place for someone in a canoe to stop and stay a while, a place that Indians knew. That's where Mom's family moved in the early 1930s. She'd have been about twelve.

Then they built the highway, and where the highway—the new means of transportation—intersected the river—the old system of transportation—people just naturally came and built and stayed. At first they called the new community Montreal Lake North Saskatchewan to differentiate it from Montreal Lake South Saskatchewan, the reservation at the other end of the lake. Then the postmaster-slash-schoolteacher shortened the name by taking the first two letters of each of the words—Montreal Lake North Saskatchewan—and renamed the town Molanosa.

It's easy to find on a map. It's at the exact geographical centre of the province.

This was where my parents made their life, raised nine children of their own — Jean, Jimmy, Dorothy, Clarence, Richard, Clifford, me, Stanley, Donny — and two grandchildren who came to live with us: Sherry-Ann, who was a little younger than me, and Garry, who was younger than Stanley.

My father integrated into the Aboriginal community, became a trapper and a fisherman, and life was good. Everything we needed came from the land: meat, fish, and put a few seeds into the sandy ground and you could grow vegetables.

That was Dad's thing, his gardens. Three of them around the house and another larger one that he shared with my grandfather where the potatoes, carrots, turnips — the basics — were grown.

These are my memories of my father, the garden and the pole fence where he liked to sit and absorb the sun; it helped his arthritis.

I have an absolute clear memory of one of those defining moments that never goes away. I would've been days away from my third birthday.

I stood in front of the house and watched her come walking up the road, carrying a bundle. I knew what was in the bundle. It was a stinky thing. Mom was coming home from the hospital, and I just stood there. I didn't move. Both my older sisters went over to see what was in the bundle, but not me.

Even my dad, he went to see what was in there, and all of them were happy to see it. Then they all went into the house together, laughing and talking, and I just stood there — mad. I wasn't going to go in there and see no stinky thing.

But Dad wasn't in the house for long. He came back out. Never said anything. Just put his arm around my little shoulders and we went over to his garden, and both of us sat on the fence in the sunshine.

And it was okay.

I was okay.

I understood, even though no words were spoken.

This was Dad's place, his garden. Here he grew those plump strawberries, and down in the back there were gooseberries and currants. The whole centre of the garden was a raspberry patch, and all across the front were his flowers.

Why? Why would a man grow flowers?

To attract the pollinators, of course, the bees and wasps and butterflies: practical.

But they were also pretty, and fit in with the little

Manitoba maples he'd imported and the Norway spruce that he had growing off to one side.

This was Dad's spot. The place where he liked to be, and it was more than sun and arthritis. This was his love.

And he brought me here, to his special place, to show me that he loved me and everything was going to be okay. He didn't have to use words. I understood. There was one person on the planet who loved me.

That stinky thing—my younger brother Stanley, born a mere nine days before my own third birthday—well, that was okay too.

There isn't a lot left of the garden. The maples are still here. They haven't grown much in thirty years, choked out by grass and weeds. The fence is gone. None of the plants that he cared for have survived: rhubarb and strawberries, even the horseradish patch has been overtaken. What was once abundance is now merely a half-acre square in the forest, and the forest is taking it back, reclaiming what was rightfully its in the first place. A man can come here, change it, make it into something else, make his living, but only the boreal has any permanence.

PENCILS

THERE'S A MEMORY: dim, not because the memory is poor, but because of the light. Kerosene lamps are not very bright. I am on the floor. All of the adults are above me and I have Dad's *Winnipeg Free Press*, a weekly paper with a socialist bent, which comes in the mail. I have a stub of a pencil and I am copying the letters from the newspaper onto a brown paper grocery bag. It's a game, it's play. But it's also an exercise designed by Dad, probably to keep me occupied.

The stub of a pencil was from Dad. He always had a pencil for me whenever I asked for one, and I asked often. The problem was I never returned them. Years later and Clarence would tell me, fill in the blanks: "Dad used to go to the store and buy pencils and cut them up into little pieces." Clarence wasn't around much when I was a little boy playing in the sand, becoming aware, learning to stand up straight, to speak. He was eleven years older. School in Molanosa went as high as grade eight. So, by the age of fourteen, he was finished school and off to work in the logging camps. He came home often. When it was time to fish, both he and Jim came home to help Dad.

I didn't see my brother Jim very often either, or my sister Dorothy, or my sister Jean, or my brother Richard. They'd finished school and gone on, out into the world. Jean became a nurse. She went north to Uranium City, left her daughter Sherry-Ann for Mom to raise. Dorothy married an American who owned a fly-in fishing camp over at East Trout Lake, and left her son Garry with Mom as well. We saw her sometimes in the summer. But she wintered in North Dakota.

Jimmy was married. He had a house in La Ronge. Richard lived with him and went to high school. I once overheard Dad say that Richard had better go to school, he'd never make a living at working.

I stop at the memory. Dad was wrong. Too bad he never lived to see it. Richard is a worker, a miner, a driller. School didn't hurt him. He never stopped having fun. Never took anything any more seriously than it deserved.

That older group of siblings finished school, came out the other end, and went on. There's a six-year gap between Clifford and me; then there was a younger brother, Stanley. There were Sherry-Ann and Garry and Donny. Donny was the baby. He got all of the attention. And nobody better hurt him. There were lots of older brothers to look out for him.

Within this cosmos of siblings, of rivalries and affiliations, gravitational forces drew some home. They stayed for a while, then spun away with the momentum of their own adult lives. The younger ones orbited around Mom, and there were two planets, Clifford and I, that were caught in each other's magnetic field and we orbited around Dad.

THE LIFE OF WATER

IT'S THOSE TWO, CLIFFORD AND DAD, who fill most of the spaces, most of my little-boy memory. Between them they taught me to read, to count, to imagine.

Clifford went to school and came home and taught me what he'd learned. Dad taught me the shape of letters.

"See, like this." And he draws the R shape, then the A and the Y. "See, R-A-Y spells *Ray*."

And I repeat, forcing my mouth to say the letters, "Awr, A, eye."

"Now you do it," and he hands me the pencil to draw the shapes of the sounds that make my name.

Dad taught me to count; to play cribbage. "Ace deuce trey four five six seven eight nine ten jack queen king." And I repeated: "Ath duth twey fo fie tik teben eigh nie den dzak ween ning."

"See, a pair of deuces equals four and a pair of fours equals eight," he said as he moved cards around on the table. He wasn't just teaching me to count and to add. He was keeping me occupied so that Mom could get her work done. There were four children younger than me for her to look after. But there was more to it than that. It was also because Dad could understand me. When I told Mom that "I lod mu pendle" and repeated three times that "I lod mu pendle," and she just stood there, shaking her head, Dad came over and told her, "He lost his pencil," and gave me another stub from his shirt pocket, and I went away with it and a brown paper bag.

"Fifteen-two, fifteen-four, and a pair is six."

A pair of sevens, a pair of eights, and a nine makes a hand of twenty-four points. I go to Dad to make sure that Clifford isn't cheating me. He assures me that my cards are, in fact, a twenty-four hand.

So that's how they did it to me, with play, with imagination; they taught me and groomed me; shaped, formed, prepared me; stood me up straight, put my feet underneath me, filled me with books and ideas; then one after the other they abandoned me here.

. . .

"DO YOU KNOW you can read minds?" Clifford sits cross-legged in front of me. "Sure, it's easy. Just close your eyes, make your mind go empty. I'm going to think of a word and you tell me what word you hear."

I close my eyes, don't think of anything, and then say, "Rabbit."

"See, you can do it. That's the word I was thinking about."

We practise again.

"Rhubarb."

And again.

"Meteor."

I like this game.

"Willows."

"Wrong, you weren't listening."

"I thought I wasn't supposed to listen. I thought I was just letting my mind go empty."

"Listen with your mind, not your ears. If you listen with your ears and you're making noise, you can't hear anything. Same thing with listening with your mind; your mind has to be quiet."

I try again, but again the word that comes is *willow*.

"You got it. Willow—not willows."

He'd done it to me, hadn't he? But why? Why play such an elaborate hoax on a little boy?

I look at the hoop in my hand, at the stub of a handle wired in place. He'd planned the whole thing, had a strategy. Of course, he needed a communication system, one that worked across vast distances, so — telepathy. That's where it started, playing a game, little brother and practise and practise and practise, until he could call me from any distance.

Maybe it started even earlier than that.

"What you going to be when you grow up?"

"I don't know."

"You should be an astronaut."

"Okay." But I was only five years old. All I knew about space travel in 1962 was what I'd heard on the radio: rockets and the Russians and the Americans and a race.

"I'm going to be a scientist." He didn't say, *I want to be a scientist* or *I hope to be a scientist.* Clifford was certain. He was going to be a scientist, as though there was no other possibility.

He put space travel into my head, then developed communications.

I run it all through my head again.

First they taught me to read and write, then to count, to add.

"Do it fast."

"Do it in your head."

"Faster."

"See, you can do it."

Clifford and Dad worked together; they must have.

They put ideas in my eager little mind.

"You should be an astronaut."

"You are the only real person on the planet."

THIS IS A waste of time. I've had these thoughts before, I've run through the entire scenario; piece by piece by piece, clicked all the connectors together... and still...

I go through it again, not because I want to, but because I can't stop.

Okay, then:

Read and write,

count,

philosophy...

Clifford and I, standing outside, looking up at a clear blue sky that's still tinged with the pale light from a sun that just set, and, without any prompting or questions from me, he explains: "You were a spirit, just a little dot of blue light travelling across the universe, and you met the Creator. The Creator is both spirit and physical at the same time, and you said, 'I want to be like that.' So you came down to Earth to experience being a spirit in a physical body."

There's that space travel again.

Ideas in a little boy's head.

Then there was all the preparation. He wasn't just teaching me how to skip rope: one end tied to a tree, Clifford at the other end, and me in the middle, developing co-ordination as I learned to jump over the twirling cord.

The lotus position:

"Sit like this, see, cross your legs, put one foot on top of your thigh, put the other foot on top of the other thigh. See, it doesn't hurt. Now put your hands on your knees. Close your eyes. Now you're doing it like a real Hindu."

Then came the hoop:

"Let's play circus. I'm the ringmaster and you're the lion. Now jump through the hoop.

"Again.

"And again."

Learning to skip rope first made jumping through a moving hoop easier. It was a set-up.

"Now for the grand finale. As you jump through the hoop, go into the lotus position while you're still in the air. Honest, you won't get hurt. You'll land on your bum here in the sand."

And I'd played along.

Because that's what I was doing: just playing with my older brother.

KNIGHTS, BICYCLES, AND AEROPLANES

CLIFFORD SHOWED ME HOW the knights in the old days jousted.

"See this?" It was a post he'd dug into the ground a little taller than my five-year-old self, with a board nailed to the top at right angles. One nail—because nails were precious and not to be wasted—and a bit of plywood on one end. The other end of the board—an eight-foot two-by-four that he didn't trim off, either because he didn't want to spend time sawing it or because he would get in trouble for wasting wood—was left jutting out on the other side of the post. "That piece of plywood is the shield. Now I'm going to come down the hill on that bicycle. That's my horse. And this"—a pole about six feet long—"is my lance.

"You watch." He took me by the shoulders and stood me off to the side. "Now you're going to see how it was done."

He came off that bit of hill on that bicycle that didn't have any tires, just bare metal rims that rattled as he picked up speed. The hill, because the bicycle didn't have any pedals and he needed the assistance of gravity. One end of his lance tucked up under his arm, the other end—"You have to hit the shield right dead centre. That's the way they did it."—out in front of the bicycle, which had a fair bit of hurry as he came past me.

And he did it.

I was the witness.

The lance did hit the shield right dead centre. A solid hit.

The shield spun away, pivoted on the single nail driven into the top of the post, and the other end of the board spun around, exactly like he planned it, exactly like he told me it was going to work. Except, I don't think he expected the long end of the two-by-four to come around so quickly and catch him on the back of the head.

. . .

HE'D ALWAYS WANTED to fly.

"Aeroplanes are easy, I can make one out of wire and plastic."

And he did. It even had a cockpit.

"See, I designed this. It's exactly the right dimensions to carry you. I've calculated the weight and the lift. Now you sit in here and I'll pull you off the roof with this rope." He probably believed it. I don't think for a second that he would have deliberately done anything to hurt me. I was the little brother—the one to be taught.

But there was no way I was going to sit in that contraption of plastic stretched over a frame of stiff wire.

Wonder where he got the wire? The plastic would have been easy: the same poly that covered the windows in winter to keep out the draft. But the wire—coat hangers, maybe. Maybe he'd raided the closet and taken all the wire hangers.

There remains a bit of what was once red roofing paper on the sagging roof of the log cabin part of the old house. The structure is in an L shape. The log house, the longer section, that was where my brothers and I had slept; the other part of the house, the tarpaper part, is a house my father bought in Timber

Bay for ten dollars, put it on skids, and dragged it with a team of horses thirty-five miles across Montreal Lake and attached it to the cabin. This newer part is divided into a kitchen at the front and my parents' bedroom at the back.

It isn't that high. Well, not now, but when I was a kid, it would have seemed a lot higher. I can see it, why he thought he could fly a plane off that roof with its low pitch. It could have worked.

"See this rock? It's the exact same weight as you." I don't know how he knew that. He never weighed either the rock or me. "I'm going to put it in the plane and you'll see. It will fly."

And he did. Put the large rock in the plane, pulled on the long rope as he ran across the yard.

And the plane did fly.

It came off the roof, lifted into the air, tilted, and made a large arc.

For a half-second there, I had actually wished that I hadn't been so chicken. I could've been up there — flying.

Then the arc turned into a dive, and the plane crashed nose-first into the sand and became a crumpled mess of wire and plastic.

And Clifford's response:

"See, if you'd been in there, you could have steered. All it needed was a pilot."

MOTORCYCLE

THE SUN HAS WARMTH to it when I step out of the shadows of the pines, out into the centre of what was once the yard, the place where I used to play, where so much happened. This is where I came into being, came into the world, came into a life, my origination.

I toss the hoop into the air, watch it spin, see the sky and the pines behind it and through it, see it reach its zenith and start to come back down. I catch it and carry it with me as I look around.

Mom's old gas-powered washing machine should still be around here somewhere — a white enamel tub with four metal legs and a place for a gas engine underneath. The wringer head, if I remember correctly, would have been stainless steel. It shouldn't be hard to spot.

She'd used it only out here, in the front yard, the metal flex exhaust pipe lying across the ground, puffing noisily. I don't think she liked it. She didn't like any technology, especially anything that used gasoline. We used kerosene lamps instead of the hand-pumped gas lamps that other families had. She liked it that way.

Probably why she didn't seem to mind that Clifford took the engine out.

Five horsepower Briggs and Stratton.

Now why would I remember that, precisely?

He probably drilled it into me.

And it had a kick-start. That was easy to remember. A gas engine under a washing machine, and you started it by stomping down on the pedal.

That's where he got the idea from, from that kick-start.

"I can make a motorcycle."

And he did.

It took a lot longer to make than the aeroplane.

His garage was a large white canvas tent at the back of the house, a shady place to work. I came to check on his progress occasionally, stood around and watched him put things together.

A bicycle, and this time it had tires with air in them and everything.

And a kickstand, so that the back tire was up in the air a few inches.

"That's so I can start the engine. It's going to be direct drive."

He didn't have to invite me to be a witness.

I wanted to be there. This was something I couldn't miss.

It was done. It had taken him days and days, but it was finally ready. The motor was mounted, chain drive to the back tire. The kickstand worked.

"Now you watch. Stand off to the side, though, don't get in the way."

He sat on it. Stomped down on the pedal and the engine came alive and the rear wheel was spinning. When he knocked the kickstand out of place, that back tire hit the dirt and Clifford and his motorcycle took off.

No brakes. Well, he had to take the pedals off the bicycle to fit the engine.

No throttle. The engine had one speed. Wide open.

He must have been doing thirty, maybe thirty-five miles an hour when he hit the back of the house.

PHILOSOPHY AND SHOELACES

I HAVE A MEMORY of riding a bicycle, fast down the gravel highway, and I know a truth, an absolute truth. Clifford told it to me. But it isn't until I am alone — my legs pumping, my heart pounding, wind and sun and sky — that it hits me and I know it: "You are the only one who is real, there is only you and God. Everyone else on the planet is a robot put here by God to keep you company."

It's my moment of awakening. I am seven years old and I am alone on a planet. I experience the birth of consciousness.

If I was seven, he was thirteen. What kind of thirteen-year-old comes up with something like that and tells it to his little brother? Did he have any idea what that was going to do to me?

Maybe he did. Maybe it wasn't just a malicious trick. Maybe he saw Dad sitting in a wooden chair, holding on, and he wanted to shield me from it. Maybe if I thought of Dad as just another robot, I wouldn't hurt so much.

No, that's too simple. I hold the hoop out in front of me and examine it closely. Anyone who could imagine something like this spaceship wouldn't make up a single-use philosophy.

That idea, that I am the only real person, infects my seven-year-old self. I have a sense of self, an absolute sense of being. I am awake, on a planet. I belong here. I have more respect for the people around me. Maybe because I see none of them as my masters, I can be benevolent toward them, treat these robots, who don't even know they are robots, with kindness, because I know the secret of our relationship and they do not.

Maybe Clifford was right. Maybe that is what he wanted me to experience: that I had no master on this planet, that I was an independent, sentient being. Maybe he planted that seed in my forming mind to help me as I became aware.

Or he was a thirteen-year-old mischief maker having fun with his gullible little brother. Tell me anything and I'd believe it. But somehow I don't think so. Whatever he did to me was intentional. It was more than that he was six years older than me. I came into this world and he was here waiting for me, waiting to teach me, to guide me.

"Roar like a lion."

And I would make the sound the best that I could.

"Hiss like a snake."

And I would put my teeth together the way he told me to and make snake sounds.

In the early 1960s in northern Saskatchewan, there were no speech therapists. There still aren't. A child with a speech impediment has to travel south to a city to learn how to speak. I had Clifford. I made lion noises to learn how to make the *r* sound, snake talk to pronounce *s*. Otherwise, I told of seeing "a cow on du wode" instead of "a car on the road." Or excitedly report that "I teen du puppied" instead of "I seen the puppies."

There's an earlier memory. A high chair, Mom, Clarence, the stove, a pot of porridge, and I know something. I know that you have to put salt in porridge when you cook it. I might be two years old and I am trying to tell these adults that someone forgot to put in the salt. No one can understand the garble of my words. I am just a little person trying to show off that I know something, and they keep putting more sugar in my breakfast.

Clifford gave me my voice, my words.

I don't remember his teaching me how to tie my shoelaces, but he must have. The memory is of his teaching a cousin a year older than me to tie his laces. The cousin couldn't, kept getting it wrong. Finally, Clifford says, "Ray, you show him how." And I untie and retie my canvas running shoe. I do it quickly, show-off style. "See." Clifford's voice is gentle. "He can do it and he's younger than you. Try it again. You can do it."

There on the north side of the house, where the grass is tall, that is where we had been sitting. I can almost see him there, the teacher, patient with his two young charges.

This house and this yard, these trees, the old garden, even the sand out front stirs memories, some of them sharp; but others, like tying shoelaces, are soothing. These are the memories that I've come back to find, to bathe myself in, or maybe to feed upon, to fill myself, to restore my soul.

Memories of Dad and memories of Clifford combine and become a memory of Clifford and Dad, the pair of them: Dad working in his garden, bent over at the waist with a hoe in his hand; Clifford with a watering can still dripping its last drops. Clifford was saying something, something long-winded, as I came up to them. Dad straightens up as I approach and says, "That's a very interesting idea you have. But have you thought about how you're going to use that idea to make things better?"

CHAIR

I DON'T HAVE TO go into the house and look at the chair again. The memory catches up to me and I allow myself to follow it. It's not as harsh as I expected. There's a gentleness to it. The memory is not even of him. I have no memory of putting on my coat and going outside; all I have is Mom's telling of it.

"He used to make me put the kids outside when he was having a heart attack. Didn't want them to see him like that. He'd sit in a wooden chair and hold on. At the end there he was having a heart attack every day."

My memory, when I force it, when I put all the pieces together, isn't much: adults talking in hushed, serious voices, going quiet when I approach, telling me to go outside and play; trips to La Ronge; then Dad is in the hospital in Prince Albert. In 1965 there were no transplants, no bypass surgeries, no stints. All they had to give him were Aspirins.

Mom goes to visit him. When she comes back, she says, "He wants to see Clifford."

That's a blow.

Why Clifford?

What about me?

I'm the one who loves him.

Why did I love him so much? Was it just because I lost him? Is this just the way my underdeveloped brain analyzed irrational guilt and grief? Or was there something more? There was, wasn't there?

Then, December 15, 1965, at ten o'clock in the morning, the only person in the world who loved me...

I came home from school at lunchtime, and Mom and Grandma were packing up his clothes, cleaning him out of the house.

I was only eight years old and I was not supposed to understand.

I had to go back to school in the afternoon.

I stood at the back of the one-room schoolhouse, three shelves of books that we called the library, I held onto the bookshelf because I didn't have the strength to stand. I stood there and cried. I couldn't go to my desk.

And Miss Sanderson taught the class, let me stand there, or left me there to sob with my head in the corner between the shelves and the wall...

I DON'T WANT to relive that.

Don't want to go through it again.

There have to be good memories here too.

Down there, down the little slope that used to seem so high, that's where Mom worked on her moosehides. Mom and Aunt Maggie laughing, and kids running all over, and cousin Virginia and I sat on the top of the rack that held the moosehide and played a game with pine needles.

But the memory of my father's funeral returns.

My oldest brother, Jimmy, went to Prince Albert with his black Chev truck and brought Dad home in the back. We had to go to the wake at the church, all of us crammed into the cab of the truck, and Jimmy got stuck in the deep snow and rocked it back and forth until he got it out again.

Then we were in the church.

Dad was in a coffin at the front.

It was nighttime and there were people there, sitting in the pews, visiting, hushed voices.

Mom lined us up: me, Sherry-Ann, Stanley, Garry; she carried Donny. We had to say goodbye to our dad. We had to kiss him. We were too short and she picked us up one at a time.

He looked like Dad, sort of, not quite; there was something missing.

His cheek was cold where I kissed him; cold and it wasn't soft anymore, like kissing a candle.

Then we got back in the truck and went home.

The funeral was the next day.

I stopped crying. I couldn't cry anymore. All the tears were gone. I was empty. I didn't sit with my family. They were all up at the front of the church. I sat with Miss Sanderson's little brother.

I can see myself there, I am above and behind the little boy in the pew next to the older boy. The older boy is about sixteen, a little older than Clifford. It's as though I am above and behind, at the back of the church, watching it all unfold. Was it the shock of it that drove my spirit out of my body?

Hey, hold on a minute—

Where was Clifford?

I search through my memories and can't find him.

Not at home; Mom and Grandma packing.

Not at the wake.

Not at the funeral. Not in the church.

They carried the coffin out of the church and the people walked behind it to the graveyard. He wasn't in that line. I was the last one out of the church. I stood on the steps and saw the people, saw my sisters walk together, saw all the people going, walking behind the pallbearers carrying—

He wasn't at the gravesite. Yellow sand against the fresh white snow, and people stomping to keep warm. More words from the preacher, then "ashes to ashes, dust to dust," and the people picked up a handful of sand and tossed it on the coffin. I did too. Thought it was my duty.

Thump.

Thump.

Thump.

Then the men shovelled, quickly, efficiently, changing off. A man shovelled for a while, then another man tapped him on the shoulder, and the first man passed the shovel over and went and stood with the people. There were a half-dozen shovelling, trading shovels, trading places. Clarence and Jimmy shovelled. I saw them. Then the hole in the ground became a mound of dirt. Someone planted a cross, and the women came up and started putting the flowers on the mound. And Clifford wasn't there.

Where the hell was he?

I notice that I'm tapping the hoop against my leg. I stop.

Where was Clifford?

Did he take off?

He'd done that before. There was the time he stole Uncle 'Dolphus's canoe. He was supposed to be in school. The memory is blotchy; overheard conversations. The canoe was missing; it had been pulled up on the shore down by the river, then it was gone and Clifford...

And Uncle 'Dolphus was upset...

Clifford came home three days later.

The clearest part of the memory is "I didn't have a paddle. I just gave that canoe a good push as I started out and I went all the way up the river by inertia."

I don't remember if I asked him or if he just told me.

There were other times.

Hitchhiked to Prince Albert. Came back. A new shirt.

"Where'd you get the money?"

"None of your business."

I've relived the memory of that funeral a thousand times in my life until now, and this is the first time I've noticed that Clifford wasn't there.

I've analyzed it.

It was such a powerful catalyst. Everything changed. One world came crashing down and a new one emerged. I became a different person.

If it had that much effect on me, what did it do to him?

How many times have I told myself that I lost the only person who loved me when I was eight years old? The man who gave me pencils, the man who hugged me and took me to his garden when I was feeling rejected because a new baby came home. The man who helped me learn to read and write and count. The only person who understood what I was saying.

What about Clifford?

What did he lose?

How alone in the world did he feel?

He would have been fourteen. He'd have spent that much more time with Dad, become that much closer.

And then...

When Dad was in the hospital and Mom went to visit him and came home again, she said that Dad told her he wanted to see Clifford. But we didn't have the money to put Clifford on the bus and he couldn't go.

Out of his nine children, Dad wanted to see Clifford...

If I felt I had a powerful connection to Dad...

I'm tapping the hoop against my leg again.

So that's why the experiments with space travel stopped.

What happened to his mind?

Did he become as angry as I did?

THERE'S A BIT of wind in the tops of the pines, a whispering, then silence.

What am I doing here?

Why'd I come back?

Is it because my life crashed, spun out of control, and came tumbling down? Did I come here to try to find some piece that I could attach myself to and maybe rebuild it? Or am I trying to find healing, fix the wounds, the grief of yesterday still fresh in my flesh, in my bones? I ache with sadness. Maybe I've forgotten who I am and I'm searching for an identity.

Who the hell am I?

I have no answer, only vague notions, something about being the son of a Swedish/Sami immigrant, a forest dweller, an Indian, and something else, something I can't name, but it's real.

BUCKSHOT

THERE'S A HOOD OFF a car, half-hidden in the tall grass. That's where we tied up the dogs. Sabre, Sporty, Queenie...the remnants of Dad's dog team, the ones he kept after he caught his feet between the sleigh runners and broke both his ankles. Not long after that he bought a snow machine.

There was one dog. A special dog.

At first, we called him only *Puppy*. He'd earn his famous name later.

Dogs weren't pets. They were workers. Dogs lived outside, tied up.

It was because of the sadness in the house, a sadness so deep you could almost see it, it pulled us all down, that Mom let us have a pet, a puppy, just one.

We could bring it in the house and play with it.

I doubt there was ever a puppy in the world that grew up with as much love and affection. Five grieving children poured their hearts out into it. He was played with constantly, and a lot of the games were rough. I remember putting him in a cardboard box and playing catch with the box.

Talk to any of my younger siblings today and undoubtedly they will remember Buckshot, the big yellow dog with the really long hair.

Mom was pretty smart. A puppy can cure grief.

But I don't remember Clifford playing with it. He wasn't part of that. Maybe he was too old for puppies. Maybe there were too many already playing with it.

But it was Clifford who named him. I remember that.

He'd grown into a young dog and had gone missing for a couple of days. There were rumours and stories. The men who worked down at the fish plant shot a dog they caught stealing meat from their cache, a yellow dog. It got away.

Then he came limping home.

Clifford picked the shotgun pellets out of his flank with needle-nosed pliers, held up a tiny handful of little lead balls, and said, "I think we should call him Buckshot."

THERE'S A CANOE on the back of my truck, a shotgun behind the seat, but that's for ducks and geese and to scare away any bear that might come wandering too close to my camp.

Where am I going to camp tonight?

I haven't decided. I have all my gear with me, just threw it in before I left, without a plan, just coming north, coming home.

The only real plan I have is that I am going to sleep on the ground. I am going to lie on the bosom of Mother Earth and feel her powers come up and heal my hurts. I might put up my tent. I might not. Depends upon the weather.

I look up, through the pine canopy. There are clouds, but they're white and puffy, no threat of rain. Rain clouds are black.

I know this stuff. I know about camping, about how to predict the weather, how to make a fire, how to look after myself, where to find food, where to find shelter, because my mother taught it to me. She insisted that I know, made sure that I had the opportunities to learn, and most of it I learned directly from her. So, later when I was a young adult and out camping with other men, they sometimes would look at what I was doing and remark, "You do that like a woman."

Women and men do things differently. I learned to trap muskrats and squirrels instead of foxes and coyotes and lynx, because that was what a woman typically trapped. They were the easy animals. Men trapped those that were harder to get, were more labour intensive.

A woman will pick up small sticks to make a fire. A man will chop down a big tree, cut it into blocks, and split the blocks into small pieces, and by the time he's done all that, she'll have the tea boiled.

A man will sleep on the hard ground, regardless of rocks or roots that gouge rib cages and numb thighs in the night. A woman will make herself a mattress out of spruce boughs, or pick a soft spot to make her bed.

A woman will wait for the fire to die down to coals before she starts cooking. A man will sear his food on the high dancing flames of a fresh fire, and eat his food charred and crisp on the outside and bloody and greasy on the inside, but he will be relaxing under a tree, licking his blackened teeth before she finishes cooking her meal.

SURVIVAL

I DON'T HAVE TO be back to work until Thursday, back south to that land of prairie. There's a loneliness down there, in that empty land, that I can't resolve, a loneliness that I tolerate until it becomes too great for me and I come rushing home; home to the trees. I've been years down there, away, and every time I come home, there's a spot where the prairie ends and the first of the big white spruce stand along the highway where I suddenly feel tired. It took many trips before I figured out what caused that tiredness. And when I did, I realized that it wasn't tiredness at all; it was relief. I hadn't noticed the tension, but it must have been in my muscle and my bone, and when I saw the trees again, I relaxed. That's what I felt as my body slumped into the seat: not tiredness, just relaxation. I was safe, among friends again.

I can survive here. If there are trees: I have a bed, I have shelter, I can make a fire, I can find food. Out on the prairie I am vulnerable, out of my element. I've often imagined what I might do if I were caught out there in the winter, a truck stuck in a snowdrift, a blown engine — if I were in the forest, it would be no big deal, simply make camp, but down there where the wind never stops, I'd have to pour gas over my spare tire and light it up.

But not today, not here. Today is warm. There's no need for a fire, unless I want to cook something. Maybe — maybe I could make myself a pot of coffee. Right here; right here in the sand in the front yard.

No — better down there where Mom used to work on her moosehides. We always had a fire going, a pot of tea nestled near the edge of the coals.

Coffee first over the blaze of fresh wood on a new fire; it boils quickly, and I have a cup while I wait for the flames to die down to coals. Then a simple meal of fried sausage and potatoes. I think of eating it straight from the frying pan, and I might have if I were in a different place, but not here, not where Mom spent so much of her time. Out of respect for the woman who taught me to do all of this, I use a plate.

The sun throws long shadows through the pine. There's a quietness to the evening, a hush. The birds and even the squirrels have fallen silent in the soft light. I sit with my back against a tree, a comfortable place where roots and ground meet in a hollow that fits my shape. The coffee in my cup has become cold, and I swirl it to stir up the grounds before I toss it away, then place the cup upside down on the ground so that nothing crawls into it in the night.

Why did we leave here?

This place, this bit of the earth where everything was provided for us, where a garden produced enough for our needs and a fishnet could feed a large family, where the animals gave themselves to us and we ate them and sold their pelts to buy salt and sugar and coffee and tea, where moosehide became moccasins and mitts and jackets.

In the late sixties Canada was moving Indians around, creating new villages and relocating Inuit people farther north. It seems that Saskatchewan wanted to be part of the new experiment and picked Molanosa. We'd been a village of about two hundred people, mostly people who had been evicted when

Prince Albert National Park was created. Now the government wanted us to move across the lake to a new townsite beside the new highway; a straight, modern highway with pavement.

A new power line followed the new highway. At some level we must have known that the new highway wasn't built for us. It wasn't for the people. It went around the people and through an ancient forest, over Thunder Hills. We heard rumours that the southbound lane would have pavement twelve inches thick, so that the trucks hauling the logs out would not break through the asphalt. The highway wasn't built for the people; it was ultimately for resource extraction. It was an accommodation for the corporations.

But the promise to the people of Molanosa was that if we moved, we would get all of the modern conveniences: electricity, phones, water, sewer, a new school. They would provide us with a sawmill that would be ours, and the men could work there and we would own the forest for ten miles around where we could cut the timber for the sawmill. The plan was explained as an opportunity.

But my family never moved to Weyakwin, the new town; the town of curses.

Swearing Bay at the north end of Montreal Lake was named after a group of white men who were paddling to La Ronge, got lost, and couldn't find the beginning of the river. Some Indians came along and found them cursing loudly.

Weyakwin: the Cree word for foul language sounded better as a name than *Swearing*. It would look better as a road sign to the tourists; but to the Cree, the meaning didn't change.

The community was still debating whether to move or stay; town meetings were being held when Clarence came home with a big truck. We loaded everything we owned into that truck that was designed to haul gravel and moved to La Ronge, to a new house.

Clarence didn't have to argue with Mom about the move. She was in the hospital.

Mom had several broken ribs where she had been crushed.

Uncle Johnny on the way back from La Ronge — Mom, Donny, Garry, and Clifford crammed into the cab of his old truck — and of course he was drunk. They said that Clifford saw it coming, grabbed Donny and Garry and shoved them down on the floor on the passenger side, and lay down on top of them.

They weren't hurt. The truck flipped—Johnny went through the windshield and hit his shoulder against a tree about ten feet above the ground. Mom was ejected, and the truck landed on her.

La Ronge wasn't a great place to live. I learned what it meant to be poor.

In Molanosa we had been rich. Mom had trapped and made money. We had gardens. We could set a net in the river and catch all the fish we needed. We had family around; I had cousins who knew me and took care of me.

In La Ronge we were isolated and dependent upon welfare.

Despite the forced relocation Mom kept trapping in the spring. There was one spring, I must have been about thirteen. I had been lethargic and sickly and prone to fainting. For no discernible reason I would pass out and fall down to awaken a moment later with a tingly face and tongue. We'd gone back to Molanosa and spent the night at Uncle George and Aunt Beatrice's before heading down the river to the trapline. The morning before we left I was walking across the one-room cabin when I fainted and fell down; my long hair hit the corner of the wood stove in the middle of the room, and everyone who saw thought I had hit my head and bashed out my brains.

Mom and I walked up the river that day on the ice. I remember the next two weeks with an unusual clarity; every detail stands out. We stayed in a small log cabin with a dirt floor and walked the river every day, checking muskrat traps. We weren't trapping hard. It seemed she just wanted to be out there doing it, to be on the land, eating good food. There is nothing as delicious as a muskrat. The meat is tender and flavourful, and once you start eating them, you want more and more until it seems you can't get full: boiled muskrat, baked muskrat, muskrat on a stick over an open fire.

It was March. The meanest part of winter was done. The days were longer and bright. There were nights when we slept outside on a bed of spruce boughs and listened to the owls hoot. We laughed often and easily, even at the owls, though I cannot for the life of me tell why the sound of owls hooting in unison was so funny. It just was.

The clearest memory is of us about a mile and a half south of the cabin. The sky was mostly blue with a few wispy clouds. The sun was to the southwest, so I estimate it was about two o'clock in the afternoon. The wind was warm and came out of the same southwest direction. The snow that time of year has melted and frozen and melted and frozen and has a different sound to it. I can remember the sound of my mother's moccasins on that snow.

She stops, turns to me, and says: "My boy, you have to learn this. You have to learn how to trap. You have to learn how to fish. You have to learn how to make your living off the land." As she says this, she waves her right hand at the forest along the river, a muskeg area covered with black spruce that grew thick together. And then she says, "In case anything ever happens to that other world."

I know what she means by "that other world." It's the modern world. It's different from this world where we are standing. This is the real world. That other world is where things like the Great Depression and the Dirty Thirties happen. Here, we have all we need.

When the two weeks of trapping were done and it was time to go home, I ran ahead of her the last mile to my aunt and uncle's house. I ran because it felt good to run; I felt alive and enthusiastic. When I got to their cabin, I didn't knock; I didn't have to. It was, after all, my aunt and uncle's house, there was no need for that formality.

On the ride back to La Ronge that evening, Mom told me, "Beatrice said that when you ran into their house today, she didn't recognize you. She said a pale, sick kid went up the trapline and a tanned, healthy boy came back."

Maybe that's where I get the conviction the land can heal. I never had a fainting spell again. The only medicine I needed was to be outside, to eat clean food, to laugh and reconnect with a world where concepts like wealth and poverty are meaningless; a place where you are as wealthy as the earth provides.

That one-minute conversation on the river ice has stuck in my head. It has shaped who I have become. I can live in both worlds. I might not be the best woodsman out here; there are others who know more than I do, but I know enough. And that knowing has given me the confidence to live in the modern world. I am not afraid. Even if bad things happen, I know that I can always come home to the forest and survive.

FORESHADOWS

THERE IS A SLEEPING bag in the truck. The night is cooler now. Where to sleep? All of the ground seems equally inviting, but I end up back in the hollow under the pine, not in the bag, just covered with it, I don't want anything between the earth and my body. I want the healing that comes from that old grandmother. I expect that I will sleep like a wolf, waking up often, looking up at the stars, checking their location, falling back to sleep to awaken again to note their new position, to watch the Big Dipper circle Polaris. There's something there, something between humans and the stars, some old connection that our spirits remember, something that's good for the soul.

I will sleep well here, with my body on the earth and my spirit in the stars.

But I don't sleep, not at first. My mind is not at rest. It wants to remember, to journey back; perhaps it's searching for its own healing.

CHEEEEEEEEEZE BURGER.

I look around for the bird that made the sound.

That was Clifford again. He's the one who told me that was what the bird was saying.

Cheeeeeeze burger. And now, whenever I hear that sound, I automatically think that's what it's saying. But I've never seen the actual bird.

It's close. So I get up and go looking for it.

Stand still and listen.

It calls again.

There it is.

No, it can't be. That's a chickadee.

Chickadees call *chicka dee dee dee*.

But the bird I'm watching, sitting high in a pin cherry tree in the soft light of evening, grey with a distinct black cap, gives the *cheeeeeeze burger* call.

Holy shit!

All this time and it *was* the black-capped chickadee.

I've solved the mystery of the cheeseburger bird.

Reminds me of Mom.

Mom knew all the birds and what they said. Only, to Mom, all of the birds spoke Cree. I should've paid attention, listened to what she said. I try to remember and all that comes is: *"Wesakicahk, omaki mitso, Wesakicahk, omaki mitso,"* the little birds that teased Wesakicahk, the trickster, in the story about when he burned his ass.

She knew them all. Hear a birdsong and she'd imitate its call with a Cree phrase, and she was so good at it that I could almost believe all the birds spoke her language, that they laughed along with her.

None of us ever learned Mom's language.

She wanted us to do well in school, and the governing thought at the time was that children who spoke Cree would be at a disadvantage to English speakers. That, and if you spoke Cree anywhere near the school, you could get the strap. Even if you were walking across the schoolyard on Saturday, if you were heard speaking the forbidden language, on Monday morning out came the length of belt.

My cousin Virginia told me that if I fell down and hurt myself during recess, I had to say *ouch* because *ouch* was English, and I shouldn't say *iyaya* because that was Cree and I would get the strap.

But I haven't started regular school yet when Clifford sends me space travelling. School would be later. First I have to get a haircut. I've never had a haircut in the six years of my little life, and my hair hangs almost to my elbows.

I don't remember my sisters' dressing me up. Thankfully, I have only stories about when Jean and Dorothy put me in a dress, braided my hair, and took me around town to show me off. One of the places they stopped was at the school. The teachers were expecting a little Johnson girl to enrol that fall.

But I do remember the haircut, vividly.

Outside. In the front yard.

Sitting in a chair, and Mom with a pair of scissors.

And my long, blond hair falling in clumps after each loud snip.

She should have known better. Indians cut their hair only when they're mourning. If you cut your hair for no reason, you can cause something bad to happen.

Crying.

An overwhelming sadness taking over.

Crying, and I can't stop.

Tears and snot and blubbering.

And I can't stop.

I want to stop.

I want to stop crying.

But I can't. Whatever it is, it's too big for me.

It's more than a haircut, way more. It's something else, not just my hair on the ground and my head feels strange. I'm getting the first haircut of my life because I am going to go to school now, and long hair is just for little boys.

She should have known better.

There was that thing with Richard.

When Richard was little, he had long hair too. His hair was so white he earned the nickname Wapoho, White Owl.

There's a story about Wapoho, the original Wapoho, the famous one.

He had two long, white braids. Mom said he was about seven feet tall and had three wives. Then the priest told him he could have only one. He went into his tent and cried all night. In the morning he came out and decided that he was going to keep the youngest wife because she needed someone to look after her. He gave each of his other wives a wagon and a team of horses, and he filled both of those wagons with things they would need.

Richard could predict things.

"Uncle 'Dolphus is coming, and he has thirty-five beaver and twenty-two mink."

And Grandma's brother would show up later that day with exactly that much fur.

Then Richard made the big mistake. He told Mom, "Uncle Jim is drowning eh." And Mom ran down to the river in time to see her favourite brother, the one she was the closest with because he was the closest in age to her, go under the broken spring ice for the last time.

Richard got a severe beating for that, as though he'd caused it.

He said he could still predict things. He just never, ever told anyone ever again.

My beating would come later.

WHIPPED

THERE'S TWO PARTS TO IT: the beating and the explanation. The whipping came first. It happened shortly after Dad died. I don't know where the extension cord came from. We didn't have electricity in Molanosa. Why would she have an electrical cable? It doesn't make sense, but it was there and she used it. She held me by the hair, her powerful hand with a fist full at the top of my head.

I remember those hands: large hands for a woman, strong from years of work, of stretching moosehides, bending trap springs, chopping wood. When Garry was fifteen and thinking he might be tough enough, he challenged Mom to a finger fight. They locked fingers of both hands, and a quick moment later he was on his knees with his fingers bent painfully backwards. He learned respect.

There's no avoiding it. My mind won't be distracted. It wants to remember the beating, so I let it go there. But the memory is like the memory of the funeral. I am not in my body. I am standing aside, watching her — out in front of the house, the sun is high, slightly to the west, she's wearing a long dress and her hair is in two black braids. I am watching her hold a little boy and flailing, over, and over, and over, until the boy doesn't have any strength left to stand, and still she holds him up by the hair and whips down with the cable.

I don't remember the pain. I try to, but it won't come back. All there is to the memory is the dislocated perspective, the view from the spirit whipped from its body.

THE EXPLANATION CAME many years later. It wasn't an apology. It wasn't even an acknowledgement that it had occurred. It was simply a story, one told during a quiet, peaceful moment when there was only she and I together: "You used to cry all the time, for no reason. You'd just be sitting there and you'd start crying. My mother told me, 'You have to beat that boy, make him stop crying or something bad is going to happen.'"

That was it. She never said anything more about it, and I never asked. We both left it there. We both understood.

Maybe something happened to her as she beat me. Maybe.

It's hard to know.

Was she following her mother's instructions? If she was, it was too late. My father had already died.

I try to imagine a forty-something-year-old woman with six children left at home, five of those children under the age of eight, and no husband. She can't leave her house or her brothers come and steal everything. The community is trying to take her trapline away from her. She's hurt and alone and she has a little boy who won't stop crying.

I suspect that something happened to her, either while she was beating me or shortly after. I have no memory of how it ended, how she finally stopped.

But there definitely was a change.

There are moments in a life, cataclysmic moments that last only a moment or two or three or four that alter the course of that person's journey. The beating didn't change me. It changed Mom. It changed how she treated me.

She never hit me again.

I passed through that moment of metamorphosis and emerged on the other side of it in a totally new environment. In that moment I earned my freedom.

RICHES

ANOTHER EXPLANATION: when I am an adult and again my mother and I are alone together, sharing a quiet moment.

"Hey, Mom, why the hell did we ever move to La Ronge?"

"Well, you remember that old house?"

"Yeah."

"There was a program, a government thing, they would help us to get new windows and doors. So I applied for it. I had to tell them how much money I made. That's how they found out I was taking you kids out of school in the spring to go up the trapline. They said I couldn't do that anymore; I had to move to La Ronge and go on welfare, so you could go to school every day." She paused, looked down, then directly at me. "The social worker said if I didn't, they'd take you kids away from me."

That's where my hatred of social workers comes from. All of them, every damn social worker who ever walked and breathed; what a pitiful excuse for a human being. They go where they're not wanted, bring their misbegotten ideas with them, and impose their values on people who were better off before social services were created. They don't come and try to persuade people; they use government power, the force of law, and the police.

So we went from being rich to poor, from Mom's being so successful at trapping that others in the community became jealous and tried to take her trapline away from her. A glimpse of a memory: Mom, home from a trappers' meeting, still seething. "I told Frank Nelson, 'What the hell do you want with another trapline? You don't trap anyway, your wife does all the trapping.'"

It must have seemed like a conspiracy to her, everyone around working in unison to force her off the land, to drive her into town, to make her poor and useless, just a woman. Trapping and making money was for men.

She used to go up the river, trapping in the winter, tell us to go to Aunt Annie's after school and wait for her. I loved Annie's house, it was full of cousins and play, and she fed us macaroni and tomato soup.

Mom came home, well after dark, and it wasn't good. She said she had walked through slush and her moccasins got wet.

I am back under the tree, lying on top of my sleeping bag as the darkness increases into night, remembering and thinking and trying to make sense of it all. She knew better. I know she knew better. If your feet get wet, you stop and make a fire and dry them out right away. Anyone who has travelled in the winter knows that.

So why didn't she?

Probably because there were six kids at her sister's house waiting for her to return, for her to get them dressed in their parkas and mitts and hats and walk them across the little community to their house, where the fire would have gone out during the day and the house would be cold, and she needed to start a fire and put them to bed before she could begin to skin and stretch the animals she had caught that day.

She had kept walking, in her wet moccasins, and by the time she arrived at her sister's house, her feet were frozen. Uncle Simeon knew what to do. He made her sit on a chair and used kerosene that had been stored outside to slowly thaw out her feet. He got her moccasins off, and all of us kids, me and my siblings and all of Annie's kids, stood around, watching. Her feet were white and solid as Simeon massaged them with kerosene. The pain must have been incredible. She never said a word, never made a sound. She wouldn't in front of us children, but she couldn't keep it from showing on her face, the tightness around her mouth as she clenched her teeth, the stern lines on her forehead, and the way she looked up from watching Uncle work on her feet to force a smile at us, so that we wouldn't worry.

That incident might be one of the reasons she took us out of school in the spring to accompany her up the trapline. She hired a babysitter, Elsie, a beautiful young woman, to come stay with us and look after us during the day. Elsie was great. She had a spirit that came alive out on the trapline, her laughter ringing in the forest. She kept us entertained and out of trouble and taught us about living outside.

But six kids are too many to watch all the time. I went into the cabin by myself, took down a .22 rifle from the wall, put a shell in the chamber, and fired it into the dirt floor.

When Mom came back that evening, my siblings told on me. "Ray shot the gun inside the cabin."

Mom had a quizzical look on her face as she very calmly asked, "Why did you do that?"

"Because I never fired a gun before."

She took me outside and showed me how. "You line up that front sight so you can see it through the notch of the back sight. Then, keeping them lined up, you put that front sight on what you want to shoot, then pull the trigger nice and slow and easy."

Either I impressed her with my ability to shoot during that short target practice session or she needed someone to help paddle the canoe.

I have two clear, connected memories: first, of shooting that muskrat—Mom was checking a trap, bent over the bow. We were at the tip of a long, narrow island a few miles north of the first cabin. The ice was gone from the river channels that flowed around the island, but a large piece jutted out between us and the channel on the other side.

I had Dad's .22, a rifle she had bought for him from the Army and Navy catalogue for seven dollars. It was a single-shot Cooey with a long, heavy forestock.

"Hey Mom, there's a rat swimming over there."

"Well, shoot it then."

"It's too far. It's on the other side of the ice."

"Just use more sight, aim high."

So I did.

Careful aim with that big rifle, heavy and steady in my hands, used all of the front sight—it covered that rat's head—then squeezed the trigger, and a rat was flipping and tossing in the water before it floated and was still.

"I got it!"

"I got it!"

"Hurry up, Mom, let's go get it."

"Just wait until I'm finished. It will still be there when we get there."

And, of course, it was, it wasn't going anywhere, a clean bullet hole through its eyes, the largest muskrat of the year and I shot it. Not only was it the largest, it was an odd colour, almost blond instead of the usual darker brown.

The corresponding memory is of selling it, standing beside Mom at Bert's General Store. There's a large pile of muskrat pelts on the counter and Bert is counting them, sorting them. I reach out and take *my* rat, separate it from the pile. Mom takes it and puts it back with the rest. "It's okay, my boy, you'll get paid for it."

Eight dollars; that's what Bert gave me — a lot of money in 1969.

The average price was five dollars, and Mom had hundreds of muskrat pelts. Not only the muskrats that she trapped; she also received a third share of whatever others trapped.

Her younger brother Johnny came up the river along with my brother Clarence. Mom sent them to trap the far end of the trapline. Her excuse was that there wasn't enough room for them in the little cabin where we were. But after they left, I overheard her say something about not wanting them sniffing around after Elsie.

Johnny and Clarence averaged a hundred rats a night. They paddled a canoe and used a flashlight. When a blinded rat swam toward the canoe, the one not holding the light shot it.

They kept Mom busy skinning rats. I heard her mumble about how her share of Johnny and Clarence's rats seemed to always be the ones that had been shot through the body, as she sewed up the bullet hole and hid her stitching so that Bert wouldn't see it when she sold it to him.

. . .

I REMEMBER UNCLE Ben again.

We were at the first cabin, and Ben had a dog team down on the river. He'd stopped at the cabin to give Mom her third share, and Mom stomped down the hill to the ice, to his dogsled, pulled back the tarpaulin, and sure enough: Ben had killed a beaver that he never said anything about.

"I knew that bastard would try to cheat me."

Either Ben wasn't as sneaky as he thought he was, or Mom knew him too well.

I don't remember how much money she made. She probably never told me. But I do remember one spring—I don't remember if it was the spring that I shot the big rat or if it was a different year—I made two hundred dollars from the rats that I shot while paddling the back of her canoe and from trapping in the bay in front of the first cabin. I might have had half a dozen traps set out there, and she didn't take a third.

FREEDOM

SOMETHING HAS A HOLD OF ME.

I am tangled.

I struggle through sleep and whatever it is that has me wrapped, sleeping bag and a rope, or a cable around my shoulders, pinning my arms.

Keep still.

Don't move.

Listen.

The night is empty of sound.

Wakefulness increases.

Even this close to equinox the nights are never completely dark; there are stars and a pale light in the northwest. The air is warm and still.

I feel for whatever has a hold of me, something stiff: a tree root, maybe, or a branch.

I carefully free myself, sit up, and examine it.

Clifford's hoop. I've somehow pulled it into my sleeping bag. I must have laid it on the ground beside me before I fell asleep.

I set it aside, well out of the way, pull the sleeping bag back up, and curl back into the hollow at the base of the tree. I note the position of the stars before I close my eyes again. It's a little after midnight.

What was I trying to do?

Go travelling.

Maybe it wasn't me. Maybe the hoop came on its own. I try to remember. I thought I had put it in the back of the truck. I must not have.

Travelling with Clifford, going, doing, being.

By the time I was thirteen, I had complete freedom. I learned to hitchhike. Simple: walk out to the highway, put out a thumb, a ride, another ride, meet interesting people on the way, and go visit Clifford in Saskatoon. Spend a few days, maybe a weekend, walk the length of Idylwyld Drive North out of the city, and put out my thumb again and go home.

I've done it so often, Grandma has a new name for me: *Saskatoon*. She pronounces it like a Cree word with the emphasis on the second-last syllable. She came and lived with us for a while after Grandpa died and Uncle Johnny, drunk again, burned down their house.

There's a memory, another one of those defining moments. But this wasn't a moment of change. It was more of a milestone or a moment of realization. Hitchhiking is always a bit of a game of chance. Sometimes you get a ride right away, and sometimes you have to walk for a while.

I was delayed getting home. Either I left Saskatoon too late or the rides didn't happen. I walked into the house in La Ronge well after dark on a Sunday evening. Mom met me with a calm "There's supper on the stove," and went back into the living room to her big chair and her beadwork. I was expecting more, something angry.

Supper was good, her usual thick soup; lots of meat and vegetables and broth. I asked Stanley in a quiet voice, "Did Mom say anything about my being away?" I hadn't told anyone I was leaving. I had simply decided on the spur of the moment to go, and then I was late getting back.

"No." He shook his head a little. "She did seem a little worried when it started to get dark, though."

I lie awake and wonder how that gift of freedom altered the course of my life. Nothing stood in the way of my growing up; there were no restrictions, only choices and consequences. I was free to go and visit my brother whenever I wanted.

Did she see that? Did she see the connection between us?

Or did she simply come to the realization that to try to restrict me would've been pointless? I was going my own way regardless, and it was simply easier on everyone not to fight with me about it.

YES, SHE GAVE me my freedom. Let me become the man I was to become. But she also played a huge role in shaping that man. I was fourteen. Not much interested in school, not much interested in anything. She insisted that I accompany her to the doctor. She told him that she was worried about me. "He doesn't seem to have much energy."

After a full examination the doctor determined that he couldn't find anything wrong with me. Told Mom: "It's pretty common for teenagers his age to be a little lethargic."

After the doctor's visit, especially whenever there were relatives from Molanosa visiting us in La Ronge, she would say, "See that boy, there's nothing wrong with him. I took him to the doctor and the doctor told me he's just lazy." It was embarrassing. *Lazy* is not something anyone wants to be called.

Then my friend Russ Merasty got a job at the gas station beside the river. If Russ could get a job, so could I. So I asked the owner, John Merriman, if I could get a job. He said, "Yeah," but because I would be working with the public, I needed to get a haircut. There were only two hippies in La Ronge in 1971, myself and James Quandt, who was a couple years older than me. I wasn't as dedicated to the cause as he was. On the way home I stopped at our neighbour Allan Thompson's house and asked him if he would give me a haircut. He did.

I was scheduled to work pumping gas after school and on Saturday.

After my first full day of work, an eight-hour shift, I came home and found that things were different. There was a place set at the table, plate, knife, fork, a small plate off to the side with a few slices of bread. "Sit down, my boy." She held the chair.

Normally the plates are in the cupboard, supper is on the stove. You get your own plate and utensils, serve yourself, and put your dirty dishes in the sink when you're done.

But today she serves me. Brings the food to the table. And while she is serving me, she says in a loud voice: "You boys—Stanley, Garry, Donny. You are responsible now to bring in the wood, take out the pail; your brother here doesn't have to do that anymore. He's a working man now."

When I was lazy, she embarrassed me. When I worked, she praised me. No wonder I became such a workaholic.

So it wasn't just Clifford and Dad who shaped me. Mom also helped, only she was more subtle about it, and it wasn't apparent to me until now, here, sitting in the dark down the little hill from the old house where my earliest memories began.

I pick up the hoop. That's all it is, a piece of plastic tubing, big enough to fit over a boy five—maybe I was six or seven—years old.

Clifford's bubble maker.

MIND EXPANSION

I OPEN MY EYES and check the stars. They've moved very slightly. I tuck some of the sleeping bag between my shoulder and an uncomfortable rough piece of root, shut my eyes, and lie listening to the emptiness of the night. There's nothing to hear, other than the sound of my own breathing.

Maybe I shouldn't have had that last cup of coffee. I'm not going to sleep very well. But coffee is just coffee and I've had it all my life. I probably got it in my bottle when I was a baby.

Memories of Mom mixing tea, half and half with milk, in one of the younger brother's bottles, and it's easy to imagine that the same was done for me.

A memory of Dad in the morning, up early, and a

pot of strong coffee. Only he and I are awake. I don't go to school yet. The ones who do will be getting up soon. I have a cup of coffee, mostly milk. We don't talk, just enjoy each other's company. A memory of the radio and a program called *Kindercorner* for children; the Lone Ranger and Tonto.

I can hear the song that started the radio show: *If you go down to the woods today, you're sure for a big surprise ... because today's the day the Teddy Bears have their picnic.*

The memory has a good feel to it, comforting. I am almost happy, something I haven't felt in a long time. The therapy is working: only a few hours in the bosom of Mother Earth and already my pain is going away.

THE NIGHT AND the sleeping bag want to take me. Thinking of my brother, how he had been, his hopes, his dreams, his ambitions — what would he have done if he had gone on? Would the scientist have re-emerged? Or would he have stayed the technician, fixing all the broken things? I realize I am going to have to learn electrical now that he is gone. I am a good mechanic; I am able to visualize three dimensions and see the inner workings of an engine, follow fuel and air flows and pistons and crankshafts, but I never paid attention to how simple things like signal lights worked. I didn't have to. Clifford was always there with his intuitive ability to find the cracked wire or the blown fuse, his ease in seeing the flow of electrons from the cathode to the anode sides of batteries.

If it involved electricity, I simply called Clifford to fix it and didn't have to figure it out for myself, and never learned. But now—now was going to be different in many ways. I am going to have to go on—on my own. My world has a big hole in it, an empty spot, a void.

I open my eyes in the darkness, laying on my side, half my vision is of the earth and shadows; the other is of the sky, treetops, and stars.

I should write Clifford's story.

The thought emerges fully formed.

But how? What would the structure look like? What voice would I use?

Biography. Maybe.

I have enough material. But writing biography requires following a strict form. Clifford would never fit in that form. He would come out all caricature, a false image of who he was. No, to write Clifford and reveal his true self requires that I write him as fiction. And he would love it, to be remembered like an Isaac Asimov character or an H. G. Wells invention.

It was, after all, Clifford who told me that there is no real difference between fact and fiction. Everything that we believe to be factual and true is just the most popular story of our time.

"Science," he said, "can never tell the absolute truth. We used to believe that the earth was the centre of the universe. Then Galileo showed us that the earth orbited the sun, then Newton added his view of gravity to the story, then Einstein modified Newton's theory with relativity, then quantum physics overtook relativity, then super strings tried to combine everything, and complexity tried to find the hidden connections. We think we have a good understanding of the universe now with billions of galaxies, but wait—in fifty years, or a hundred years, they are going to look back on what we think we know and say, 'How quaint.' And a hundred years after that, the story that replaces our story will be replaced again. All we have is the best story we can come up with to explain what we think we know, and all the while we know the story is wrong. If we ever found the true story, science would come to an end."

So, if I write Clifford, I write him as fiction, as a fantasy, as a thought experiment. I close my eyes and the earth and the sky disappear. The warmth of my sleeping bag wraps around me and sleep pulls me under, into that half-world where reality and fantasy mingle in a place where coherent thoughts disintegrate.

Clifford is here somewhere in this mist. I can hear his voice, his words, then the sound of his laugh, somewhere off in the dark. I begin to wake up again, somewhere in that middle world between sleep and consciousness, and I am five years old again.

CLIFFORD'S GAMES WERE much more interesting than anyone else's.

"See, bubbles. It's easy, just soap and water and blow on the straw and you can make bubbles."

And it is fun.

I run around the yard, even in the house, with a cup of soapy water and a straw, and make bubbles, lots of bubbles.

What was he teaching me?

"Everything alive has a skin. You have skin, animals have skin, trees have bark—that's just another kind of skin. Water has to be alive because it, too, has skin."

"Water doesn't have a skin."

"Sure it does. That's what you're making bubbles out of. Water skin."

Then he shows me. A glass of water . . . slowly, very carefully, fill it until it is overfull and the water is actually above the rim of the glass.

I can see it.

Proof.

Water has skin; that's why it doesn't flow over the edge.

Water is alive.

"How big of a bubble can you make?"

So, I practise. Long, steady, slow breaths. I can make a bubble as big as my head.

"Bet I can make a bigger bubble than you."

"Can not."

"Can too."

"No way."

"Watch, I'll show you."

Then out comes the hula hoop with a piece of wood wired in place for a handle. Mom's washtub full of soapy water. And Clifford can make big bubbles, huge ones. I can chase them, I can catch them, throw them in the air. They're bigger than me.

"How'd you like to go inside one of those?"

"Really?"

"Yeah, really. If, while I'm making a bubble, you jump through the hoop at the same time and go into the lotus position while you're in the air, your feet won't break the bubble."

See...

Set up.

Set up.

Set up.

Run...time it so I'm there exactly when the water skin begins to bend inside of the hoop...easy...into the air, lotus position, duck my head. The hoop passes over me.

I'm inside a bubble.

Up to this point, I can almost believe it. It could actually have happened.

I've even figured out how he made the big bubbles, the secret ingredient.

Corn syrup.

Mom's corn syrup. It was in a white bottle with a picture of a yellow cob of corn on the label. She used it for baking and sometimes she mixed Mapleine, imitation maple flavour, with it, and we used it on pancakes.

Yeah, that's all it took: corn syrup, soap, a washtub, and a hula hoop.

Mix six parts water, one part dish soap and glycerine, or corn syrup, together—let it set overnight, and anyone can make huge bubbles.

It took a while to find the recipe. I must have been almost twenty-five before I discovered it. One part of the puzzle solved.

But there's that other part. The part that I still don't believe actually happened. Or I haven't figured out how he did it.

"Do you believe in God?"

"I don't know."

"I don't mean the old white guy with a beard, sitting on a throne in the clouds, who drops manna with one hand and throws lightning bolts at you with the other. I mean the god who is part of everything."

"I guess so."

"Okay, then. I want you to hold onto this."

He dips an eagle feather in the washtub and gently pushes it through the bubble.

"Careful now. Just pull on it nice and easy, and the bubble won't pop."

It didn't.

I sit inside a bubble with a sticky, wet eagle feather in my palms.

Parts of the memory are dimmed by time, there's a bit of vagueness to it all. Except the next part. This I remember as though it happened only a few minutes ago.

"What goes faster than light?"

"Nothing."

"Think; what goes faster than light?"

Nothing goes faster than light. Light is the fastest. He proved that to me with a flashlight. Right after he proved that sound travelled and that sound was slow. "Watch Dad splitting wood. See that. You can see him hit the block and then, a little later, you hear the sound. That's because sound travels." Then he points at a white streak across the sky. "See the jet? You can see the jet long before you hear it. That's because the jet travels faster than sound. It leaves its sound behind."

A flashlight in the dark, a beam against the cabin wall.

"The light comes out of the flashlight, right?"

"Uh huh."

"So it has to travel from the flashlight to the wall, right?"

"I guess so."

"So how fast is it?"

"I don't know."

"One hundred and eighty-six thousand miles per second."

So, why is he asking me what goes faster than light when he's taught me about Einstein and proved that nothing goes faster? Light is the fastest. Einstein said so.

"Think."

Very carefully, slowly enunciated, patient. "Think...What. Goes. Faster. Than. Light? Think."

It's an impossible question. My mind goes blank.

"Think." His voice is gentle, encouraging.

"Think."

A word emerges in my empty head: "*Thought*. Thought is faster than light."

"Right. You're doing good. Now something else. Remember solar sails?"

I remember. If you took a sail into outer space where there is no atmosphere, no gravity, and the sun shone on it, it would move because the light was moving, and when the light hit the sail, the sail would move because there was nothing to stop it. The same as if the light were wind. I remember.

I also remember: "You can move things with your mind. Close your eyes. Hold on to that eagle feather and think yourself into outer space."

So I did what I was told. Thought myself into outer space.

I hear him in my head.

"Do not open your eyes."

"Okay, I won't."

"If you open your eyes, you might get scared and pop the bubble. Then you'll be stuck up there."

"Okay."

"Right. Now think yourself back down here again."

How gullible could I have been, how completely trusting? He convinced me that I had gone into outer space. That I had travelled in a bubble spaceship propelled by thought energy.

I should have opened my eyes. But I didn't. I played along, because that's what it was all about: play. It was just another one of Clifford's elaborate games, and I was a little boy, happy to have someone play with me.

If it had been only the one trip into outer space, I could have written it off, let it go. There would have been nothing there, just an older brother playing tricks and I had figured out how he'd done it. But there was that other trip, the next one, that I couldn't quite get my head around.

THE NIGHT IS an envelope of darkness that surrounds me, a big envelope filled with stories that I fall into.

I was fourteen and hanging out with him, just hitchhiked down for the weekend.

We were in his apartment in Saskatoon. "Here, try this," he'd said.

"What is it?"

"LSD. Expand your mind a little. Let some truth in."

So I did. One tab of purple microdot.

"There are two ways that this can go. You can journey around, enjoy yourself, experience everything in a new way, or you can freak out and have a bad trip. Both are in your mind. Your choice."

Clifford's apartment: well, it wasn't really an apartment, just two rooms in an old house, a hot plate and a fridge in one room and a couch and his bed in the other, down the hall a bathroom shared with the other tenants.

The LSD melted the walls and warped the table, brought some colour to the drab surroundings.

"You doing okay?"

"Yeah, I'm fine. A bit weird, but what the hell, nothing wrong with weird."

"Wanna go out? Think you can handle it?"

"No problem."

So we went tripping downtown Saskatoon on a bright sunshine summer morning. Found the park by the old hotel beside the river. Met some friends of his, long-haired friends and a girl with flowers woven into her hair and a long, cotton dress who danced barefoot with me in the grass and laughed a tinkle laugh that turned all the trees into glass, and the sun came through them and the colours danced in time to the music.

I don't remember her name, but I remember the taste of the wine and that I thought it was pretty special that the bottle touched her lips just before it touched mine.

Another time:

"Mescaline isn't like LSD, it's smoother. Organic. I think you'll like it."

That was a road trip. We hitchhiked down to Regina. And mescaline isn't like LSD; the hallucinations are more subtle and you have to be careful that you don't confuse the images with reality. LSD images are bright and contrary to reality and easy to differentiate. Mescaline images look like they might even be real; the road continues on in front of you, indefinitely leading to paradise as though you might be walking through a painting you once saw hanging in somebody's living room, and it doesn't matter whether it's real or not; it's good to walk on the road to paradise with your brother.

"You have to be careful with this; you're really open to suggestion. Someone might say something and you'll think you can do it. Just stick close to me."

"But you're high too."

"Yeah, but I've been here before."

I wasn't sure whether he meant the mescaline or Regina and it didn't matter. I was fourteen years old and out in the world, and the world was a good place to be.

Another memory in the jumble: we were in front of a television, in someone's house, they were watching the moon landings and debating whether it was a hoax. Did they actually go to the moon, or did NASA stage the whole thing to win the space race with the Russians?

"There's no way to tell from the images," a know-it-all proclaimed, a young man with an attitude who took a counter position to whatever direction the conversation threaded. "We've never been to the moon before, so no one knows what it really looks like. It would be a simple matter to set up a Hollywood production."

"Ray knows what it looks like." Clifford started to laugh. "Tell them. Is that what the moon looks like?"

"What's that?" someone asked.

"Oh, he's been there. He knows what the moon looks like. Just ask him, he can tell you." But he's laughing too hard for anyone to take him seriously.

NOW I'M AWAKE again, fully awake; sitting up in the night. The hoop is where I'd laid it, on the ground out of the way. There was that second trip. The one where he sent me to explore the moon, the one that I can't explain.

I review it:

In the bubble, cross-legged, eagle feather in my hands, eyes closed:

"Think yourself to the moon."

"Okay."

"Now open your eyes."

Below me, a pockmarked, barren landscape; I am close enough to the surface to see the gravel, the grit, and the rocks. Above me, a large blue planet with white swirls. I have only a few seconds to look around before I hear:

"Close your eyes again and think yourself back here."

And I am back in the front yard and he pops the bubble to release me.

How did he do it?

Kaleidoscope.

He'd been playing with those—a long tube with holes punched in it to let in specks of light—and put my eye to one end to see a constellation.

Maybe.

Maybe while I had my eyes closed on the journey to the moon, he'd put a big cardboard box with holes in it over the bubble and painted it on the inside so that when I opened my eyes, I would think that I was on the surface of the moon. And then when I had my eyes closed again for the return journey, he'd taken it away and hidden it.

But how the hell did he know what the surface of the moon looked like, and why did it match up with the images from the lunar lander five years later?

An elaborate hoax.

And I've never satisfactorily figured out how he'd done it.

"Good one, Clifford." Words spoken into the darkness.

There is no answer from the night.

A puzzle.

I speak again to the silence, with confidence: "I will figure it out."

THE STARS

THE BIG DIPPER HANGS a little more toward the east, partially hidden by the trees. I can see the two stars on the end that line up with Polaris, my navigation pointers. I know where I am.

I learned that from him, about the two stars lining up. Much later, we were young adults, standing roadside in the dark: "Remember when those stars lined up perfectly with Polaris? Now they are off a little."

As soon as he said it, I did remember: "Yeah, they used to line up exactly. What the hell is going on?"

Clifford laughing so hard he can barely get the words out: "You just remembered something that happened five thousand years ago."

"Bullshit. I remember. I have a clear memory of

those stars." I point them out, one—two—three. "They lined up." I am positive.

"They did. But not in your lifetime. That's cellular memory. Your DNA is remembering. The last time those three stars lined up was five thousand years ago."

It seemed impossible. The memory was too clear, like it was only a few years before, or maybe even the last time I'd looked at them.

"We can all do that, you know. If we try. We can remember what actually happened in history if our parents or grandparents or great-grandparents were there. Their cells are in us and those cells carry memory."

Memory, memories, remembering; I can't trust my own brain to remember. My first clear memory, the farthest back that I can go, is of being about one year old. I calculate the age by the year we moved up the hill, the year after the flood. The water from the river came up higher than anyone ever remembered, almost to the back of the house. There are two memories here. One is of Clifford showing me how high the water was in the well, almost to the top. The other, the one I told him was my very first memory, is of opening the door to the log house at the bottom of the hill and coming in from bright sunlight and having to wait until my eyes adjusted to the dark. The image that I call my first memory is of Mom and Aunt Maggie sitting at a table by a window to my right.

Clifford pointed out that was impossible. If the window had been to my right, that would have been the north wall, and there were no windows on the north wall. No one ever puts a window on the north side because that's the cold side.

He was correct. There was no window on that side of the house. But that was my memory. That was the image that came up, clear and concise: Mom looking younger than any other time; Aunt Maggie laughing, which was not unusual. Aunt Maggie was always laughing.

My memory was flipped. It was a mirror image. It had been stored like a photo negative, and when I retrieved it, it came up backwards.

I look back up at the stars, reconnect with the two on the end of the Big Dipper that don't quite line up with Polaris. North hasn't moved. It's still there above the old house. I am here. In a good place.

Knowing where I am also informs me of who I am.

I belong here — this place, this earth, this time.

I am connected — this life, this galaxy, this universe.

I remember, shortly after I got out of the navy, Clifford and I shared an apartment in Saskatoon.

I worked at the Key Lake Uranium Mine during the exploration and development phase, three weeks at the mine, one week out. The week out was mostly a party, lots of alcohol and eating in restaurants.

Clifford worked as a radio and television repairman in one of the last shops in the city that still repaired televisions. It was a dying profession. He'd really miscalculated that one. He'd thought that electronics was going to be the cutting edge of the technology of the future. It ended up that televisions would become disposable. No one would pay to repair one when it was cheaper to just buy a new set, with colour and a bigger screen.

I'd gotten off the plane after a three-week stint in the mine, in my early twenties, with the vigour, strength, and testosterone that my age determined. Three weeks of running dozer, eating sand and dust, working with a big iron machine that rattled my bones and probably my mind as well — I was ready to head for the nightclubs, raise a little hell.

Clifford had the microwave oven torn apart and spread all over the kitchen table.

"What's wrong with it?" I tossed my packsack onto the couch.

"Nothing. I just need a piece out of it."

"Fuck. I paid good money for that. Couldn't you steal the parts you need from work?"

"No, they don't make this kind anymore."

I understood what he meant. That microwave, or, rather, what was left of that microwave, was an older model built when it was believed that we needed a little CANDU reactor to warm up a cold cup of coffee.

"Aw fuck!" is what I said, but *Oh well* is what I meant and what Clifford understood me to have said. I had never really much liked that unit anyway. It made me nervous. I knew enough about radiation from my navy training, how to prepare a ship to survive the fallout of a nuclear attack, and from the little bit of radiation safety training they gave us at the mine. I'd always stood well back from that microwave whenever it was on, when it growled and rattled. It had a good, solid steel case, but I doubted that it provided much shielding from the damaging effects of high-intensity microwave radiation.

"So what're you building?"

"Rocket."

"What the fuck you need a rocket for?" Even though I had not trusted it—it was, after all, me who had bought it—if he was going to take it apart and make something else out of it, it should be something we could use.

He stopped fidgeting with whatever it was he was fidgeting with, looked up at me, looked me directly in the eyes, and asked, "You ever hear of a microwave rocket?"

"No."

"Well, neither has anyone else. This is going to be the first."

Okay, so then he had me interested.

"Tell me."

He rubbed his beard, smiled; there was a mischief in his eyes. "Fundamental physics. Remember Einstein?"

"Yeah."

"Well, he was wrong." He switched off the oscilloscope. The one he borrowed money from me to buy and never paid me back. Doesn't matter; between him and me, money flows without meaning. The glowing green screen with white grid lines faded to black. He disconnected the lead wires, coiled them up, and placed them on top of the set. "Before I can explain it to you, you have to be in the same head-space I was when I figured it out."

"And where was that?"

"Peyote."

Peyote? Really? That was almost a mythical sub-stance. LSD was easy to find—street acid that was mostly strychnine. Mescaline showed up once in a while, but that wasn't real peyote; it was a synthetic almost-peyote. Most of what was out there was PCP, Angel Dust, and I never did really like it. It slowed me down too much, felt like I'd smoked embalming fluid.

"Who's got peyote?"

"Al."

"How much?"

"It's free. Al's got religion."

"Since when?" I really doubted that our most reli-able dealer would ever give anything for free. With Al, there were never any samples, no checking it out first to see if it was any good. As with all dealers, you paid before you got stoned because no one would ever pay for a stone they already had.

Clifford answered, "Since he started using peyote."

. . .

AL'S APARTMENT, AVENUE F SOUTH, wasn't far from the river and within walking distance to the Friendship Inn, where a guy could get a bowl of soup with a chunk of day-old bread every day at noon, hang around after, hang out with all the other peoples of the street. Clifford ate here often; not because he couldn't afford his own lunch—he liked the people, liked their company, their conversation. Here were the long-haired, the remnants of the revolution, mingled with the old and wine-bottle wise.

Al lit a cigarette (yes, you could still smoke in public spaces then), leaned back in his chair, all four hundred pounds of him. I worried about the chair. He eyed me, his head tilted to the side, doubt written all over his face. "I don't know . . ." he started.

"It's alright," Clifford offered. "He's okay."

Al sat forward, the legs of his chair hard against the floor, leaned across the table, and looked intently at Clifford. "I don't mean any disrespect, don't get me wrong. It's about enlightenment, and, yeah, I'd like to see the whole world enlightened. But your brother here, and I get it, I seriously get it, you want to coax him along, that's cool, that's really cool. But look at him, short hair, shaved. Look at how he dresses. He has *military* written all over him. You can't fix a mind like that."

Clifford leaned forward as well, elbows on the table, his face squarely in front of Al's, an empty soup bowl between them. I may as well have not been there; neither looked at me. "Al, why do people join the military?"

"God save the fucken queen. Rah! Rah! Rah! To be the leaders on the path of destruction."

"There's no rich kids in the army. They're all like Ray. They join up looking for a career. That's how they suck them in. Military people are just ordinary people."

"They might have been ordinary people when they signed on the line, but man, that's one big brain fuck they go through; and when they're done with them, after they've changed them, remade them in the image of the soldier, taught them to shout 'Yes Sir, No Sir, Three bags full Sir,' they're not one of the people anymore — they're something else, something different, they become them and see us as the other. They only know *us and them*. Rah, Rah, Rah Us — Fuck, Fuck, Fuck Them. March in ranks of four, salute, shine your fucken shoes." Al paused, took a moment to breathe. "You know what Einstein said. He said that anyone who put on a uniform and marched in rank was disqualified from having a brain; all they required was a naked spinal column."

If you're arguing with Clifford, it's not a good idea to throw out an icon like Einstein to support your position.

"You're quoting the father of the bomb." He put it out there, put it into the space between his face and Al's face.

Al opened his mouth — either to speak or to swallow.

Clifford held up a hand. "It's okay," he soothed. "I like Einstein too. He was pretty cool with that 2 percent solution to the draft and all he did for peace, but we have to be careful. The establishment throws his name out all the time, as though he were the Jesus or Buddha or something of the modern era. Every time they want to convince us to go along with one of their ideas, all they have to say is, 'Einstein said,' and the people go, 'Oh yeah, you can't argue with Einstein. If Einstein said it, it must be true,' and they keep us going in that same direction."

Al weakened. "Okay, I'll give you that."

"Now Ray here" — Clifford didn't look at me, just indicated with his hand in my direction, kept his eyes locked with Al's — "he wasn't in the army, he was navy. There's a difference. He knows about oceans, about big water; there's depth to his understanding, whether he knows it or not. And anyway, they didn't get to his brain. They couldn't; he was stoned most of the time he was there."

Al was softening, but he wasn't about to relent. He didn't have any words left. He sat back, put some distance between himself and Clifford, and shook his head. The answer was still *no.*

"We're not asking for free," Clifford pressed. "We'll pay the going rate."

Al's answer, slow and resolute: "You can't buy salvation."

"You had to pay to get it; nobody gave it to you for free. We'll reimburse you your costs."

Ultimately Al relented, though I doubt the money was the deciding factor. I did end up paying what I suspect was a little less than street price, probably Al's wholesale price. We followed him to his apartment, Clifford and I in my truck, Al leading the way on his motorcycle. He made that 500 Honda look tiny; kind of reminded me of a circus bear on a bicycle.

He lived in a basement suite with a private entrance around back of an old three-storey wood house that had once been the home of one of Saskatoon's more privileged society, and was now divided into revenue generators for some slumlord.

The peyote had a rubbery texture and not much for taste, like dried-out mushrooms. The couch I sat on didn't have much spring left to it and it swallowed me into its lumpy core. Its legs had long since been broken off, and it sat on its box frame so that my knees were about equal height with my chin.

Al sat on the floor, cross-legged, his shirt open and peeled back off his shoulders so that it hung behind him by his elbows. He mumbled a chant that some-one might have taught him, or perhaps it was of his own making.

I fell into the rhythm of his words, listened to its beat, until the beat of his song became tuned to the beat of my heart, which sounded louder and louder in my ears. Slowly the room filled with corn grow-ing up out of the carpet, brilliant green stalks with golden tassels.

Clifford came through the cornfield, reached down a hand to help me rise; led me, slowly, carefully out of the apartment and up the stairs, out into the backyard of tall grass and discarded furniture, mattresses, and broken tables, surrounded by a weathered fence that still had most of its boards standing upright.

"What?" I looked around.

"Rocket," he answered. "Microwave," he reminded me.

"Oh yeah."

"I want to show you something."

"What?"

"Space," he said.

I looked up. The afternoon was getting late. Evening wouldn't be too far off. The sky was clear. Maybe when it got dark, we could see the stars.

"No, not outer space. This space." He held his hands up and apart.

I looked at his hands; they looked like they might be made of stone. I looked closer to see the runes carved in the palm.

"No, no, no." He waved them in front of my eyes, and they blurred. "Space, I want you to see space."

I wasn't getting it. I felt myself starting to rise up, lighter than air, I was a balloon about to float away.

"Stand here." He held me by the shoulder, turned me toward the back fence. "Look at that tree, but don't look at the leaves; look at the spaces between the leaves until you don't see tree but see only treeness."

I did as I was told, stared toward the west, focused on the pale smoky blue between the flittering green, watched as the image slowly changed dimensions and I began to see the tree's silvery aura.

"Got it?"

"Yeah," I answered slowly.

"Okay now, look here."

I didn't want to. I liked the tree with its glow.

"Here," he commanded.

I looked. He was pointing toward the ground.

"Look closely. Space is a thing, and like all other things it's made of waves — electric waves, micro-waves, radio waves, even time waves. Do you see it?"

"Yeah." And I did, I could see them: long, skinny waves, almost grey in colour. I looked up to where they were coming from. The sky was filled with long, thin, wavy threads, some coming down toward me, others travelling criss-cross in all directions.

"Now look down here."

I looked.

"See here. See where they hit the ground and bounce back."

"Yeah." I didn't have much for words; my world was too full of wonder.

"See how the wave coming down meets the wave bouncing back up."

"Yeah."

"See how when the trough of one wave matches up with the peak of another wave, they cancel each other out."

"Oh yeah, cool." I watched, fascinated, as space waves disappeared two by two before my eyes.

"So, check it out. Look up."

I looked up.

"See how many more space waves there are above you."

There were, many more, light grey and even a bit tan in colour, thick tangles of wavering threads.

"And see, closer to the earth, there's fewer of them."

"Okay. But what's it mean?"

"Means there is less space closer to the earth than above. That's how gravity works. It's not the earth sucking on you. It's all the space above you pushing you down."

My perspective immediately shifted; I could feel the weight of space on my shoulders. It made perfect sense. Less space closer to the earth because the reflected waves cancelled each other out meant more space further up meant my feet were stuck to the planet.

"So, to make a rocket, all I have to do is replicate

the frequency of space so there is less space in front of the rocket than behind it."

"Hey, that would work." I watched the waves bouncing off the ground, coming back up. I reached out to touch one. It wriggled through my fingers.

"Want to see something really cool?"

"What's that?"

"Check out these waves. See how they're long without much modulation?"

"Uh huh."

"Look close, see the very tiny waves on top?"

"No..." I couldn't see what he meant.

"Remember when you were in the navy and out at sea, how on the ocean there were big waves and on top of the big waves, there were smaller waves."

I remembered an undulating sea of shallow swells, our ship slicing through, and, yes, of course, there were the ripples on top of the swells. I looked again at the space waves in front of my eyes, at the long, easy curve of them. I looked closer and, sure enough, there they were, tiny waves, ripples in the clean flow of the space thread.

"Know what that is?"

"No." I didn't.

"Time." His voice close to my ear.

"Time?" I looked into his bearded face, through the wavering space waves between us.

"Yeah, since time is part of the space wave, when the space waves cancel each other out, time disappears. That's why time runs slower down here than up there."

I knew that. Not about the waves, but about time running slower closer to the earth. Wasn't that long ago they put a super-sensitive clock on top of a water tower and one on the ground, and, sure enough, the clock on the ground ran slower.

I followed a wave with my eyes as it came down in front of me, watched the tiny time waves on its surface. "So what causes time then?" I wanted to know. My mind open, expanded to allow all possibilities.

"Motion," he answered. "Time is the result of motion, or, I don't know, maybe time allows motion. Anyway, the two are together. If you were to stop all motion in the universe, then time would stop. If you cool something down to absolute zero so that the motion in its atoms comes to a stop, its time would stop. That's one of the reasons we can't get to absolute zero. Hey, check it out. You have your own clock inside of you."

I looked. Sure enough, there it was, in the centre of

my chest. I unbuttoned my shirt to see it better. Made mostly of polished wood, it was beautiful. I watched the second hand sweep around, looked at the gears and wheels spinning.

"Check out mine," he said.

I looked. His was made of stainless steel, shining with its own glow. I felt a tinge of jealousy. Why was his made of stainless steel and mine only of wood? I looked back at mine, noted that the gears were ceramic. Somehow that made it better. Ceramic is in many ways superior to steel. It can take more heat.

"That's going to be the hard part," he said.

"What is?"

"Time."

"For what?"

"For the rocket."

"Oh yeah," I remembered.

"Finding the right modulation so that I can regulate its speed."

"I thought you were going to cancel out the space waves to make it move."

"That, and time together. If I can get time to run slower in front of it than behind it . . . Well, we'll see how that turns out."

Somewhere in a world filled with flowing space

waves, somewhere in the afternoon that became evening that became night—somewhere I lost Clifford. I wandered the riverbank alone, found people to trip with. Met a woman who held my hand. I tried to show her the space waves, but her wine and marijuana trip didn't allow for insight.

I found morning, or morning found me, in Ila's bed. Or maybe her name was Ida. I don't know, Ila or Ida, I lay awake listening to the sound of her breathing, not quite snoring, not wanting to be in bed anymore and not wanting to leave before she woke up. That would have been rude.

Ultimately I made my way back to the apartment. Clifford was drinking coffee. He had a cup in his left hand and he was putting things away, slowly, without any deliberation, just sort of cleaning up after.

"You missed it," he said.

"What's that?"

"The rocket. Launched it this morning."

"Really?"

"Yeah, I figured out how it all works."

"How all what works?"

"Space, gravity, reality, all of it. Remember those space waves I showed you?" He coiled the wires leading to the oscilloscope.

"Oh, I remember alright." I must have still had some peyote in my system because I saw a brief glimmer of them at their mention.

"Those are the fundamental building blocks of everything in the universe. It's all about how much energy is applied to them. Do you know the electromagnetic spectrum?"

I didn't.

He explained. "It's all about how fast the waves vibrate. If they're vibrating very fast, they're gamma radiation; a little bit slower and they're X-rays; slower and they become ultraviolet; then we're into the visible light part of the spectrum. Think of a rainbow."

In my present state, it wasn't hard to visualize.

"The rainbow has all the colours arranged based on the speed the light wave is vibrating: violet, blue, green, yellow, orange, and red. If we slow the wave down some more, we get infrared; a little slower and we get microwaves; then the slowest are radio waves. But all of them were first space waves. It just depends upon how much energy is added to make each one." He took a sip from his coffee. "But I knew most of that already. What I figured out last night kind of surprised me."

"What's that?"

"It has to do with light. We know that light can be either a wave or a photon, and that a photon is a type of particle. So if light can be either a wave or a particle, and light is just space with more energy applied, then space, too, must be either a wave or a particle. We don't have a name for space when it takes that form, so I made one up. I call it a *spaton*.

"And just like when space is a wave, the energy we add to it when it is a spaton changes it. Depending on how much energy is added, it can become an up quark or a down quark."

"Whoa, whoa, you're losing me."

"Quarks. That's what the protons and neutrons in the atom are made from."

"Yeah, I know, but slow down."

"There are six different types of quarks, depending on how much energy each has. To make a proton you need two up quarks and a down quark. To make a neutron you need two down quarks and an up quark. Basically, quarks are the building blocks of atoms."

"And if a quark was originally a chunk of space, or, as you call it, a spaton, then everything in the universe was originally space."

"You got it."

I was slowly getting my head around it. But I still had a question. "So what's that got to do with your rocket?"

"Well, the spaton part and the fact that all matter was originally space were just a bonus that came from the idea that space could be either a wave or a spaton. It had nothing to do with the rocket. But it helps in understanding space in all its forms.

"As for the rocket: once I figured out the speed that space waves were vibrating at, it was easy to convert microwaves back into space waves, and once I knew how to make space waves, I knew how to cancel them out, so there was less space in front of the rocket than behind it and the space behind pushed it."

"So what speed do space waves vibrate at?"

He looked at me for a long second before answering. "You'll have to work it out for yourself. I can't tell. If people found out, they'd use it to kill each other."

Now I became skeptical. Son of a bitch brother was fucking with me. Again.

"So how high did it go?" My question sounded more like a test.

"Don't know. It never came down."

. . .

I LIE IN the darkness, my back curled, listening to the sound of my own breathing, remembering. I don't know which I regret more: believing him in the first place, or missing out on seeing that rocket go up.

TRICKSTER

MOM TOLD STORIES ABOUT Wesakicahk, the trickster, how, whenever he did something, it always turned out messed up. She told the traditional stories that her grandmother had told her when she was our age, stories about his tricking the ducks and geese, and the loon telling on him, and how he burned his ass on a hot rock to teach it a lesson.

The wonderful thing about our trickster was that we could also make up stories about him. Clifford said that in the olden days, when someone wanted to confess something to the camp, they would wait until evening when everyone was around the fire, telling stories, and they would make up a story about what they did and blame it on Wesakicahk. Clifford also said that was why Wesakicahk left us. He saw hard times coming for the people and he didn't want to get blamed for it.

"But Wesakicahk will come back," Clifford said. "He will be here in the future." Then he told me the story that he had made up:

Kayas—Clifford started the story with the Cree word that means *long time ago*, but since it is always used at the beginning of traditional stories, maybe it means *Once upon a time*—Wesakicahk had forgotten most of the teachings of the Grandfathers. He knew a little. He still remembered a few things but not much; he remembered what a rattle was for, and he still had a little bit of magic left in him. But most of the things from the Creator, Wesakicahk had forgotten.

At that time the scientists had learned a few things. They thought they knew just about everything. They had an idea about what they called *space glue*. They knew that most of reality was emptiness. They knew that the atoms were held together by something, but they did not know what that something was. And they knew that if they took an atom apart, the pieces would still be connected by some mysterious force. This mystery had the scientists confused, and they wanted to find out the secret of the force.

Well, one of the scientists was more determined than all the others. He wanted to be the one who became famous for discovering the secret of existence. The mystery frustrated him. The more frustrated he got, the angrier he became. Finally, in great anger, he succeeded in breaking the bond between atoms. It sounded like cloth ripping. From somewhere he heard someone say *ouch*. He had put a hole in reality itself.

The scientist became very afraid because the hole he had created started to grow. As a hole in anything will get bigger by itself, so did the hole in reality. And there was no way to stop the hole from getting larger. It looked like a black ball that kept growing. Anything that went into the hole disappeared, because its atoms could no longer be held together. Since all things are made of atoms, when the force that holds them together is destroyed, the atoms, being very small, drift away into the nothingness of the hole.

The scientist tried putting lead around the strange hole. Lead was the most dense element that he knew about. Well, lead slowed the hole from growing a little, but since the hole was created by destroying the force that held atoms together, even lead, which is made of atoms, could only slow down the hole from growing.

Strange things began to happen. Animals came to the hole like a moth to a flame. Insects buzzed at the window of the laboratory and crawled under the door. Birds tried flying into the building. Animals from the forest came into the city to be near the hole. Any animal that was able to get into the hole did, and disappeared because their atoms were no longer held together.

The people found out what was going on because the scientists could not keep it a secret with all the animals on Earth acting strangely and trying to get into the laboratory. The people were very afraid when they found out existence was in danger and the scientists could not save it. Some scientists said the hole could be used to get rid of nuclear waste, which they had a lot of in those days, but the people no longer trusted the scientists and would not go along with the plan. Anyway, the scientists could not be certain what would happen if nuclear waste was put in the hole.

Something had to be done. The animals would not stay away from the hole. All day eagles soared over the laboratory, waiting for a chance to get inside.

Lions tried to escape from zoos. A big herd of ele-phants drowned, trying to swim across the ocean. Whales were throwing themselves onto the shore along with fish and turtles, and the people were afraid that if they did not do something, there would be no animals left on Earth. The people were mostly afraid because bears and wolves were walking into the city, and they were scared to be outdoors.

They decided they would send the hole far out into outer space. Perhaps even to the end of the universe.

Wesakicahk asked if he could steer the spaceship that took the hole far away. He told the scientists that he would steer the spaceship for as long as he was alive, because it would take longer than many lifetimes to get there, and then he would point the spaceship toward the end of the universe before he died. The scientists agreed to let him go because it was important that nothing happen to the spaceship that carried the dangerous hole until it was very far from the earth. If the hole was free to grow, it would swallow up the earth and the moon and even the sun. Mostly they let Wesakicahk have the job because none of them wanted it.

Wesakicahk was alone in the spaceship, far from

Earth. He was very lonely. He used his rattle and sang an ancient song.

He prayed hard.

He had given the remainder of his life for Creation and would die alone out among the stars to take the hole far away from the people he loved. He was very afraid of death and was very lonely. He prayed with so much sincerity that Eagle appeared in the space-ship with him.

"What are you doing here?" asked Wesakicahk.

"I am a spirit," answered Eagle, "and I have taken the form of this sacred bird so that you can see me and speak to me."

"Ohhh," said Wesakicahk, figuring it out. "Spirit in the form of a sacred bird; you have wings, you can travel across the universe — can you take this hole to the end of the universe for me so that I can go back home?"

The spirit bird answered, "The end of the universe is not very far away. In fact, the end of the universe is in the hole you are trying to take there." Then the spirit eagle disappeared.

Again Wesakicahk used his rattle and his song, and again the spirit returned, this time in the shape of a sacred wolf.

Wesakicahk asked it, "Brother, I cannot get my feeble brain around the idea that the end of the universe is the hole I am trying to take there. Can you help me get rid of it?"

"No," refused Wolf. "Humans made the hole; it is up to them to get rid of it." And it left.

Once more Wesakicahk sang in time to his rattle and prayed, and again the spirit returned, this time in the shape of Buffalo.

Wesakicahk asked the buffalo spirit, "How can humans mend the hole they ripped in Creation?"

"Do like the animals," answered Buffalo. "They love Creation so much they are willing to give their lives for it."

After the buffalo spirit left, Wesakicahk was alone in the spaceship. He thought about going into the hole if he could be certain that would mend it. But it was a big gamble. What if he misunderstood what the spirit had meant? What if he went into the hole and it just became bigger? He had to be sure before he gave his life because he only had one life and didn't want to waste it. So he rattled, sang, and prayed one more time.

The spirit returned, this time in the form of a child.

Wesakicahk's face showed his confusion.

"Sure," said the spirit. "Humans are sacred animals too."

It took Wesakicahk a moment to get his head around that idea. He just sat there, thinking. Finally he asked in a sincere voice, sincere because his life depended upon it, "Why will the hole be mended if I go into it? Does it demand a human sacrifice?"

The spirit child laughed, a little giggly sound. "Humans believe we are the most important of Creation because we are the most destructive. The animals tried to give their lives to the hole because they love Creation. They came to the hole to give their love. They loved so much they were willing to give their lives for it."

Now Wesakicahk was very confused. He asked the spirit, "How can love mend a hole in existence? Isn't love just an emotion? How can it fix anything in the real world, like holding the atoms together?"

The spirit child laughed even more. When it finally settled down enough, it said, "Existence is love. The force that keeps the atoms together is the Creator and the Creator is love. It was only because the scientist was angry that he was able to put a hole in the Creator, and it was the Creator who said *ouch* when the scientist put a hole in her."

So Wesakicahk filled his heart with love for all of existence, which is the Creator, and the hole closed itself back up. Then Wesakicahk turned the spaceship around and came back to Earth.

Clifford said, "From that we learned to love all of Creation, and why we try so hard to live in harmony with the animals and plants that are our sacred brothers and sisters in Creation. We are all held together by the same force that keeps our atoms from drifting apart."

GROWTH

I CHOOSE TO REMEMBER the good times; it's what he would have wanted. Maybe the reason he tried to teach me so much was so that I might know something. Maybe I am wrong to doubt everything he said as another one of his hoaxes, tricks played on the little brother.

I HAD COME back from the mine to our apartment, and Clifford needed money. He should have just asked to borrow a hundred, but instead he set me up.

"You're looking good," he greeted. "Quite a bit bigger than when you left."

"What are you talking about? I'm not bigger."

"Sure you are, considerably. I can prove it."

I was skeptical, but cautious. He was up to something. "Okay, prove it, then."

"Well, let's make a little bet. How about a hundred dollars?"

Careful now. I flashed back to when we were children and it was our job to do the dishes, Clifford washed and I wiped. He made the chore into something fun. He would bet he knew how many forks or knives or spoons there were, and the bets were never small, a hundred or a thousand dollars. He kept track of how much I owed him, and the amount added up to millions of dollars. Not that I could ever pay my gambling debt at six years old. "That's okay," he'd say. "You can pay me when you're an adult."

I knew to be cautious. "Exactly what is the bet?"

"I bet one hundred dollars that I can prove you are considerably larger than you were three weeks ago when you left to go to work." His face was blank. A poker face. I couldn't see anything in it.

I thought about it for a moment. It was only a hundred dollars. I had a whole paycheque in my pocket. And it was intriguing.

"You're on. Prove it."

"Why is the sky blue?"

"What's that got to do with anything?"

"Everything." He went to the big armchair and sat down, legs outstretched.

This was obviously going to take some time. I sat on the couch across from him. Waited.

"The reason the sky is blue is because space is moving toward us, carrying the light."

I just shook my head. Didn't say anything. It would all come out.

"Remember the big bang?"

"Not really, a little before my time."

He smiled. "Yeah, about fourteen billion years before your time. Anyway, *the big bang* is the wrong name for the beginning of the universe. The theorist Fred Hoyle was criticizing the idea when he accidentally came up with it. *Big bang* gives an image of a mortar shell or an atomic bomb going off. It wasn't like that. The expanding universe isn't debris flying away from an explosion."

"What is it then?"

"The origination of the universe was a spore that spontaneously began to grow. The universe is growing, not exploding. It's actually more like mycelium or maybe mycelia, not sure about that. Anyway, we know the universe is expanding because of the red shift of distant galaxies. You know red shift–blue shift?"

I shook my head. Not too sure about that either.

"Think about the sound of a car. You spent a lot of time hitchhiking, right? Remember when a car was approaching you, it sounded different from the way it did after it passed and was heading away from you? There was a difference in pitch?"

Yeah, I remembered.

"Well, that was because as the car came toward you, the sound waves it put out ahead of itself were shorter, and when the car was going away from you, the sound waves were longer, kinda stretched out behind it."

"So?" I wanted him to get to the point.

"Well, light does the same thing. If an object, say a distant galaxy, is moving away from you, its light waves will be longer and will look red. If a star or a galaxy is moving toward you, its light will look blue."

"And?"

"And so we look out at the universe and most objects that we see are red shifted. That means they are moving away from us. If they're moving away, then at one time they were closer. If we go far enough back in time, they must have all been in the same place. We speculate that the beginning of the universe was at one time about the size of a pinhead. It's this predominant red shift that we see that starts the big bang theory.

"Now if we look at the theory and accept an infinite universe, we find that there are galaxies that were created at the big bang that we will never see because the light from them can never reach us. They are moving away from us faster than the speed of light."

"Impossible." I knew this much.

"Impossible that anything can move faster than the speed of light, you mean."

"Of course."

"Well, they are not moving faster than the speed of light in relation to the space around them. The space in between us and them is growing." He paused. Looked around the apartment, nothing there; looked out the window to his right at the tree in front of the building. "Think about 'Jack and the Beanstalk.' Remember Jack on the magic beanstalk and it's growing really fast while he's on it. The branch just above him is moving away, but not as fast as the branches farther up. And the very top of the beanstalk is growing away from him fastest of all."

I got the image. Maybe from a cartoon. But I could see it.

"Like that. You're on the beanstalk or you are in space and it's growing. In relation to the beanstalk you're not moving very fast at all."

"Okay, I get it. But what's that got to do with anything?"

"You got it?" He nodded toward me, confirming.

"Yeah."

"So since the big bang the universe has been expanding like a giant mushroom, and it is the space in between the galaxies that is growing, driving the expansion, right?"

"If you say so."

"I say so. No argument yet?"

"No, I accept what you say: the universe is expanding because space itself is growing exponentially." As far as I could tell, my money was still safely in my wallet.

"Okay, now let's switch from the macro to the micro level. You are made of atoms, which consist of protons and neutrons that form a nucleus, and electrons spin around it. And the distance between the nucleus and the electron is relatively large, and the distance between the individual atoms is extreme. You are, in fact, mostly empty space. About 95 percent empty space."

I could feel myself losing my hundred dollars.

"So if all space is expanding since the big bang, then the space between the atoms in your body is also expanding and you are larger than you were three weeks ago. We don't realize that we are growing, because any ruler we have to measure ourselves is also growing at the same rate. It's puzzled scientists as to why, if the universe is expanding, our galaxy doesn't seem to be expanding too. They came up with the idea of gravity to explain it, that the mass of the galaxy creates enough gravity to keep it all together. They're wrong. It just doesn't look like our galaxy is expanding because the earth and the sun and all the planets are expanding at the same time."

He held out his hand.

I paid up. It would have been easier if he didn't have that smirk on his face as he took my money.

BLACK HOLES

THE MEMORIES COME, one after the other, rapidly. Clifford needs to speak. The night is still, and I sit up, my back to the tree. The sleeping bag wrapped around me. Sleep is not happening. I wonder: Are these his memories that won't leave me alone?

"WHAT'S UP WITH YOU?"

Clifford seemed a little down. He hadn't said much in the previous three days, lost in his own thoughts, wandering around the apartment. He'd even cleaned up, something that was not in his habit. To Clifford, dishwashing and floor sweeping and putting things away were too mundane; he usually had more important things to occupy his mind and his being.

This morning when I woke up, he'd already washed the dishes. He hadn't put them away; they were still in the drying rack by the sink, and the stack of books by his chair had been returned to the bookshelves. Something wasn't right.

"Worrying," he answered with one word.

"About what?" I hoped it wasn't about money. I was running a little low.

He stopped halfway across the living room and just stood there, looking out of place. He pulled at his beard, a bit of a tug that made his face even longer. He tilted his head slightly over to one side and said carefully and deliberately, "I think I might have accidentally brought about the end of humanity."

"Well, that's good. I thought you needed money or you'd gotten someone pregnant."

"I'm serious." He was facing me, his hands now on his hips. He still looked out of place, standing in the middle of the room. "I might have destroyed the earth."

He was sincere. I could tell that. It was obvious that he believed what he was saying. I wasn't just playing along with another one of his crazy ideas when I asked, "So how did you start Armageddon?"

"It's not going to end like that. There isn't going to be any last big battle and angels coming on winged horses with flaming swords. I fucked up. I think I might have royally fucked it."

I could hear the hurt in his voice, but I couldn't believe that my long-haired, hippy, eccentric brother had brought about the end of it all. It couldn't be as bad as he was making it out to be.

"So how'd you do it?" I needed to know before I could dissuade him of his obviously flawed ideas.

"Remember that microwave rocket I made?"

I looked at the empty space where the microwave used to be on the kitchen counter.

"The way it worked was to cancel out space in front of it so that the space behind it pushed it."

"So?" I deliberately sounded skeptical.

"Sit down and I'll explain it to you. Pay attention. I'm only going to tell you once. You might have to explain it to someone else, so I'll tell it very simply."

I took a chair. He stayed standing, like a professor in front of a class or maybe a prophet to the multitude.

"Space is a thing. I showed you that it's made of waves. The opposite of space is a void, and, no, I'm not thinking in binary terms. There are a multitude of ways of knowing, but to understand space, you have to understand no space. You either have space or you have a void. A void is nothing. Absolutely nothing, no dimensions, no time. Imagine a void..." He used his hands to mime what looked like a box in front of him: four sides, a top, and a bottom.

"Here is a void. If I take a single photon of light—" He held an imaginary photon between his thumb and forefinger and placed it inside the imaginary box. "When I put it in the void, it is both nowhere and everywhere at the same time, because in a void, there is no position. Now let's place a particle in the void." Again he made hand gestures, a particle between thumb and forefinger into the void that I was beginning to see. "We don't know how big that particle is. It might be as small as an electron or as big as the universe. We have no way of knowing because we have nothing to compare it with. Right?"

I nodded. Yeah, I got it.

"So we have to put another particle into the void twice the size of the first particle so that we have something to compare it with, but even then all we can say is that particle a is half the size of particle b. Either of them might still be larger than the universe, and we haven't gotten anywhere other than to say that everything is relative. We don't know how far apart the particles are because without space between them, they don't have position. In a void they could be touching or infinitely far apart.

"So space must be something. It keeps things apart. If there was no space, you and I would be touching because there would be nothing between us. Or we couldn't carry on this conversation because we would be on opposite sides of the universe. So space does two things: it keeps us apart and it keeps us together. It gives us position. We are where we are only because space is real." He paused for a moment. Collected his thoughts. "Now, for time. We have to go back into the void with our two particles. In a void there is no time. We don't get time until we move one of the particles. Time and motion are the same thing. Without motion there is no time. But time only exists between two things. We can say that particle b is moving at a rate relative to particle a. If we add another particle and move it, then we change time again and we have two different times in relation to the third stationary particle. If we move out of the void into the universe with galaxies and stars and planets in orbit, time becomes very complicated."

"That can't be right." It didn't make sense to me. "If every moving object has its own time, then you and I are moving and we have the same time."

"No. There is a time difference between you and me. It's just so small that we don't realize it. We're both on a planet moving through the universe, and that bigger motion creates a bigger time that we are caught in. Anyway, that's not important." He waved away the idea with his hand. Discarded it. "What's important is that we are not in a void; we are in space, and an object moving through space will create waves. Time is a wave, and the bigger the moving object, the bigger the wave; and all those waves are travelling across the universe like ripples on a pond when you throw in a pebble."

"So," I interrupted, "what's that got to do with you destroying the earth?"

"Patience." He held up a hand. "I'll get to that. First I have to explain dark matter."

"What's that got to do with anything?"

"Nothing. But I'm going to explain it anyway because it all fits together." He took a step toward his right as though he were arguing from a different perspective. "Space is something, right?"

"Yeah." He'd already said that. More than once.

"So, there's outer space, we all understand that. But there is also space between the atoms. In fact, about 95 percent of matter is empty space. That Higgs boson thing, that's a mistake. Even if the boson gives mass to particles, it doesn't account for the solidity of the space between the atoms. That solid space is the missing dark matter that they are trying to figure out. It's right there in front of them all the time.

"You know about weather, right?"

Of course I knew about weather. It was one of the things that I paid attention to. I was getting pretty good at predicting it too.

"Well, you know about high and low pressure systems in weather."

I nodded. Yeah, I knew that.

"Well, the same thing with space. Close to the earth space is at a lower pressure and farther out space is at a higher pressure. When the pressure of space becomes great enough, it starts to resemble mass. When we add more energy to space, the spatons turn into quarks and become real mass. Dark matter is when space itself is just really thick."

It was making sense. "Okay, I get the dark matter, and probably dark energy as well. That would be the driving force behind the expansion of the universe."

"Sort of but not quite. Ever heard of particle, anti-particle, emergence, annihilation?"

"No." I hadn't heard this one.

"That's the newest theory. That a particle and an antiparticle emerge out of a vacuum spontaneously and then recombine and annihilate each other, and the force they give off drives the universe. It's wrong because it's too complicated. The universe doesn't work that way. The universe is simple. What happens is that space itself coalesces and forms the basic element helium, the simplest atom. If you combine four helium atoms together, you get hydrogen; four hydrogen, and you get oxygen; and so on until you fill the whole periodic table."

He stepped back to where he had been standing originally. "But it's not time or dark matter or dark energy that I am worried about. It's space and putting a hole in space. That rocket that I sent up created a void in front of it and the space behind it kept trying to push it into the void."

"Whoa, whoa, whoa," I interrupted. "I thought you said, when you made it, that all you were doing was altering the space waves in front of the rocket. You never said anything about making a void."

He deliberately spoke slowly and clearly: "When you cancel out the space waves in an area, there is no space left. That is the very definition of a void.

No space. It works on the same principle as gravity. Space pushes us down on the planet. Space pushed my rocket into outer space. Basically it was being pushed away from the earth at the same acceleration as gravity. So it was moving at about 9.8 metres per second per second. The thing is that it didn't have anything to stop it, so it just kept going faster and faster without a limit."

"Until it got to the speed of light." I knew something.

"No, the speed of light depends on space. Light travels at 186,000 miles per second through space. If there is no space, light doesn't go anywhere."

"So your rocket didn't go anywhere either because it moved into the void in front of it."

"The rocket never went into the void. It was always on the cusp of the void, with space trying to push it into the void, so there was no limit on its speed. It would keep travelling and keep accelerating until the battery went dead. That's the only thing I can think of that might save us. If the battery died before the rocket created too large a black hole."

"Now you lost me. A black hole is created by the collapse of a neutron star to a super-dense mass with extreme gravity. How can a void make a black hole?"

Clifford shook his head. His face said, *How can you be so dumb?*

"When a star goes supernova, it doesn't collapse in on itself. It's more like an atomic bomb. It's an explosion. Not an implosion. And if it explodes with enough force, it can tear a hole in space itself. That's what a black hole is. It's a hole in space. It's a void. The reason things disappear into black holes is because they lose their space. Any object falling into a black hole will lose the space between its atoms and disappear. All of the quarks that make up its protons and neutrons will be nowhere and everywhere at the same time. They lose their position. Even light. Remember, a single photon in a void will be everywhere and nowhere at the same time, which is an oxymoron because there is no time in a black hole." He was starting to sound as if he was going into a rant.

"Our galaxy spins around a black hole. It's not being sucked in by the mass of the black hole. It's being flushed by the mass of space beyond it. It's like the black hole is the bottom of the toilet and our galaxy is just the turds spinning around and around."

"No, sorry, now you lost me. Why is the galaxy spinning around the black hole at its centre?" This wasn't making sense. Or he was telling it too fast and I missed something.

He paused, stood a full minute looking down at the floor, and seemed to be collecting his thoughts. Then he looked up, took a breath, and began to speak slower than before. "So you know the earth orbits around the sun, right?"

Yeah, I knew that.

"And all of the planets likewise orbit the sun in the same direction as the earth."

No, I didn't know that. But now I did.

"If you look down on the solar system, so the earth's north pole points upwards, all the planets orbit in a counter-clockwise direction. And all the planets rotate on their axis in a counter-clockwise direction, and all the moons around the planets orbit their planet in a counter-clockwise direction, and the rings of Saturn spin around Saturn in a counter-clockwise direction. And all the planets going around the sun are like the rings around Saturn—they extend out on the same plane. That's because all the planets and all the moons and all the rocks in the asteroid belt are caught in a whirlpool of space around the sun."

"You sure about that? All of them orbit the sun in the same direction?"

"Yes, I am sure." His tone was as definite as his words.

"And all the planets rotate on their axis in the same direction?" I needed to double check.

"Except Venus. Venus rotates clockwise but that's because it got hit by an asteroid or something that sent it spinning backwards. Venus's rotation is slowing down. It will eventually stop and begin to rotate in the proper direction in a few million years. But it's not the direction that's important. Direction could be a fluke. What's important is that they're all on the same plane."

I was beginning to see it, beginning to see the solar system in a whirlpool around the sun. "But what causes it?"

"Oh, same reason we have gravity on earth. Space waves colliding with the sun are consumed, creating low space pressure." He was talking fast again. "Michelson and Morley..."

"Who?"

"Late in the last century, two guys named Michelson and Morley did an experiment with light that seemed to prove once and for all that space did not exist. Actually, back then they called it the *Ether*. They knew the earth was going around the sun and assumed that it was moving through the Ether. The result of the experiment was that the earth was not moving in relation to the space around it." He scratched his head vigorously with both hands, maybe to massage his scalp, maybe to get more blood to his brain.

"Of course the earth isn't moving through space. It's moving *with* space. That's why the result of the Michelson–Morley experiment was nil. Things can move through space, can even go against the current of space, same as an aeroplane on a windy day, or a ship cutting across ocean currents."

I put out a challenge: "Where's your evidence?"

"Weather patterns," he answered. "Because space is spinning around the earth in a counter-clockwise direction, the majority of the winds on earth are from west to east. That's at a surface level. If we go deeper, we encounter continental drift. The continents are moving very slowly around the surface of the earth counter-clockwise as well."

He paused. Took a step to the right again. Changed his mind and stepped back to where he had been. "You got this?"

"Yeah, got it." I replied.

"One more thing. When we look at black holes, we

see jets of energy coming out each end. Black holes are always in the shape of a sphere and they always rotate. So, if a particle—and there must be trillions and trillions of particles going into these things—if one of them is inside the black hole, in the void, it has no position. The only places with position on a black hole are the two poles."

"Stop." I held up my hand, palm toward him. "Two things: What do you mean by jets of energy coming out of black holes, and what do you mean black holes have poles?"

"The energy jets have been observed. They haven't been properly explained, but they have been seen."

"So what causes them, then?" I knew he didn't want to be interrupted, but he was going too fast for me to follow.

"I told you that black holes rotate, right?"

I nodded. Yeah, I'd heard that part.

"Well, they rotate in a single direction like the earth and that rotation is on an axis that results in the black hole's having a north and south pole. Now the thing is, if you stand a foot away from the north pole, you are moving in a circle around it. Even if you are half an inch away, you are moving. But if you could find the exact north pole, the precise point, the exact axis the black hole rotated around, you would not be moving. You would have position. So any particle inside a black hole that accidentally comes into contact with either the exact north or exact south pole of the black hole immediately gets ejected because it found position, and it's those particles being ejected that make up the jets of energy that we see."

He calmed himself down a bit. "Now back to that damn rocket. It travelled straight up, creating a void in front of it. It created a long black hole from here to I don't know how far into outer space."

"Whoa, sorry. So how does the void become a black hole again?"

He sighed. I could see his exasperation. He was obviously thinking, *Why aren't you getting this? It's simple.* But when he spoke, it was with patience. "I created a void by getting rid of the space in front of the rocket. All of the space in front of the rocket was cancelled out. Got it?"

"Yeah."

"Well, a void is just another word for black hole. They are the same thing. The only reason I use the word *void* is to differentiate it from space. We either have space or no space. When we have no space, it's a void. When we have a big void surrounded by space, we call it a black hole because it's basically a hole in space. Anyway, the one I created in front of the rocket will be only about four inches across, but its overall size will depend upon how far up it went. I went back and checked, and I can't detect anything, so maybe space pushed in on it and it's much smaller than the four inches.

"But here's the kicker. If space pushed in on it one way, then it probably pushed in on it linearly as well. That means that it might not be long and skinny, a scratch in space. It might have become a sphere, I don't know. Maybe the faster the rocket went — and I'm pretty sure the battery lasted until well after it exceeded the speed of light — maybe at that speed it did more damage to the space it was travelling through."

I consoled, "But it would be pretty far away from Earth by the time that happened."

"True, except that one tiny end of the black hole points directly down on this apartment building. In fact, it would be right overtop of your bedroom. I launched it from that corner of the roof."

"Okay, so . . . I still don't get it. How did that start Armageddon?"

"If I in fact created a massive black hole out in

space, and the track that created it points back here, I'm worried that the black hole will follow the track of the rocket back down here."

"Why would it do that?" I was looking at the ceiling.

"Path of least resistance is what I am worried about."

WE NEVER DID resolve the black hole thing. It never happened or it hasn't happened yet. We did move out of that building not long after, and we kind of split up. We went our different ways. He got married, had three kids, broke up with his wife, and ended up back in La Ronge with his children. He kept doing experiments and what I began to consider as simple silliness, nothing of importance.

I got married, had two children, and ended up living just outside of Prince Albert. I kept working at mining and logging, but having a family, raising children, meant that my life was more controlled, more purposeful. I didn't have time to use my mind for things like black holes and space travel and Clifford's world of fantasy. I had important things to do, like make money to support my family.

RACIST

I DON'T REMEMBER WHAT we were doing in Prince Albert. Just a chance get-together. Both in town at the same time and decided to go check out our favourite restaurant. I do remember that we walked there, through downtown, Central Avenue and the panhandlers. We were passing a pawnshop, and he stopped and looked through the window at the collection of rings.

"Getting married?" I asked.

"No, I'm looking for a ruby."

"What do you want a ruby for?"

"What are rubies used for?"

I didn't know; couldn't think of anything.

"Shine a light through a ruby and all the light waves are concentrated into one laser beam."

"So, next question: What do you want a laser for?"

"I don't want a laser."

My confusion kept me silent.

He explained. "Light is a wave. But light isn't the only thing that's a wave. It's just one tiny part of the electromagnetic spectrum. Radio waves, microwaves, X-rays, gamma rays — they're all waves. I want to see if I can focus these other waves the same as a laser."

I let that sink in, with all the connotations; tried to imagine a concentrated beam of gamma rays. The only image my brain could come up with was a *Star Trek* phaser and Captain Kirk blasting aliens. Then a thought, remembering that space itself, according to Clifford, was just another wave. "Hey, could you make a tractor beam?" I was still on *Star Trek* and towing a disabled USS *Enterprise* with a beam of light.

"I don't know. Hadn't thought about that," he answered. "I suspect it would work kind of like magnetism."

We were walking again. None of the rings in the pawnshop window had a red gem inset. We continued toward Tilley's Restaurant a few blocks west of downtown Prince Albert, in a rougher part of town.

He'd been silent as we walked and I was in the mood for a discussion. We hadn't seen each other for a while and I missed our conversations. "So, tell me. How does magnetism work?"

"Space waves."

I didn't respond. No need. It would come out.

"Take any material and arrange its molecules so that they line up and you get a magnet. The way it works is, because the molecules are lined up, space can move through the material in a straight line. Usually space waves just go in any direction and are a jumble. But when you line them up, they begin to flow."

"Hold on. I thought space waves bounced off material. Isn't that what causes gravity?"

"Some of the space waves bounce off the surface. Some go deeper before they hit something to bounce back. Remember, even things that are solid are mostly empty. Same thing with a magnet—space waves move through the empty gaps between the atoms all in the same direction. You know that opposites attract and likes repel."

Of course I knew that, everyone does.

"The reason is the space waves coming out of the magnet. If you put two magnets together so that the north and south poles are together, the space waves flow from one to the other. When the waves are inside the magnet, they're compact; when they jump the gap between two magnets, they stretch out to make the jump. The waves act like a spring when it's stretched; they want to take their original shape again and contract. That's what pulls the two magnets together."

Okay, I could see it: waves that acted like coil springs. A two-dimensional image of a spring kind of looks like a wave. I could see it stretched out and contracting. But I still had a question. "So, what causes likes to repel?"

"Same thing. If you force two magnets together so that the space waves coming out of each of them meet head to head, the waves are compressed and, again like a spring, they want to take their original shape and push back."

We walked on, mostly in silence, and I let myself absorb this new information.

We were sitting in a booth in Tilley's Restaurant when he bluntly stated: "You know you're a racist."

"Bullshit!" I called him on his naked statement.

We had just sat down in anticipation of one of Tilley's huge meals. She had taken our order: coffee, soup of the day — tomato macaroni — big burger, and fries. We both knew that when the meal was over, we would both order pie and ice cream. We've been here before, many times over the years. If we are in Prince Albert at the same time, it's where we go. Tilley knows us and likes us. We eat. She likes to feed people and it makes her happy when two skinny guys come in and order her biggest meal.

Her big burger is no quarter pounder. It makes a quarter pounder look like a snack. She has to make her own buns to match the handmade patty and all the lettuce, cheese, bacon, tomato, onion, relish, and mustard. And it isn't served on a plate. A plate is too small. She serves it on a platter with a pile of french fries and a heap of coleslaw.

"You can't help yourself." He spooned his soup.

"Bullshit!" I wasn't buying it.

"I can prove it."

"No way. Not a snowball's chance in hell." He wasn't going to get away with anything as absurd as calling me a racist.

"You pay for lunch if I do?"

"You're on. And if you can't prove I am a racist, you pay."

Elbow on the table, hand stroking his beard. "You

are a racist because you live in a racist story and there is nothing you can do about it. Everything is story. You are story, I am story, the universe is story. Figured you'd know this. You're a writer."

I am a writer. Have always been a writer, ever since Dad showed me how to copy the letters from the *Winnipeg Free Press* onto a brown paper bag with a pencil stub I borrowed from him and never returned. There was a time when I was about seven, I was already going to school and bringing books home with me. I was sitting, reading a simple kid's book, and Dad came by. He never said anything; just placed a copy of Harper Lee's *To Kill a Mockingbird* by my elbow. It was a struggle to get through. I had to force myself to understand all of the words, all of the complex sentences. I probably stayed with it to the end only because it was Dad who gave it to me. I never figured out why he gave it to me. Was it because it had children in it my age and he thought I would enjoy it? Or was he pushing me to read at a higher level?

As a teenager I wrote poetry. Still believe the world could be saved by an army of thirteen-year-old poets, with all the love and caring and hope they generate.

Clifford also encouraged my writing. When I came home on leave for Christmas from the navy, his present was a little book: *Writing in General and the Short Story in Particular* by Rust Hills. I've been exploring the craft of storytelling ever since. When I am at work in the mine, driving a haul truck and waiting for my turn for the loader to fill my truck, I write down a few lines, and then while I am driving the truck to the dump area and back, I am thinking up the next few lines.

I wasn't sure where Clifford was going with this. "What do you mean, 'everything is story'?"

"You're made out of DNA, right?"

"Yeah."

"And DNA is a four-letter code. A, C, T, and G. With that four-letter alphabet we write every living thing on the planet. When we understand this language, we will understand life. We will know the story.

"This table is just a story." He taps it with his knuckles. "It's made out of atoms, but it's the space between the atoms that gives it solidity. All that holds this table together is the story we all agree upon. It's the uncertainty principle in science. We can know the velocity of an electron or its position, but we can't know them both at the same time, so we can't know anything absolutely. Combine that with the observer effect, that we change things by observing them, and the only reason that anything exists is because we are conscious of them. We, in fact, make it up. It's the story we all agree upon. Reality is a story. That's why Einstein said, 'Reality is an illusion, albeit a very persistent one.' He also said, 'I refuse to believe the moon is not there when I am not looking.' He wasn't convinced it was all story. He believed in objective knowing.

"So let's accept his reasoning for a moment. This table" — Clifford raps it again — "is solid, it's an object. We can say that it is objective, but any description of it must be subjective because we are humans and we can't help but be subjective."

"Hold on, hold on. You're getting too carried away. I'm not entirely subjective. I have objective, rational thoughts."

"Do you? Are you sure?"

"Of course I'm sure. I can be completely objective and put aside emotion and irrationality."

"Let's start at the beginning. Shortly after you were born, someone put a nipple in your mouth and squirted warm milk and you heard sounds.

Somewhere in your brain a neuron fired and connected with a neuron on the other side of your brain, creating a pathway, and you inferred a connection between the taste of warm milk in your mouth with the sounds your mother was making and you began to infer language.

"Throughout early childhood you learned an incredible amount. Each new thing you learned built upon the earlier things you knew. When you encountered a new experience, you inferred meaning to it based upon those things you already knew. Gradually you built up a body of understanding. Through grade school, then high school, out into the world, you kept learning and are still learning. Each time you encounter something new, you infer meaning to it based upon those things already in your head, and all those things in your head were things you inferred."

He tilted his soup bowl to spoon out the last tomato and macaroni.

"Problem is that because you inferred the meaning of everything that you know based upon things you already knew, if you made a mistake, if you made the wrong inference anywhere along the way, going all the way back to the taste of warm milk in your mouth, everything that followed would be wrong because the basis it was built upon was wrong. You don't know anything with absolute certainty."

"And neither do you."

"And neither do I. Difference is, I know that I don't know anything. Everything I think I know is stuff that I made up. So I am very careful with the story I tell myself."

"And the bullshit story you're telling yourself today is that I am a racist. I'm still calling you on that."

Tilley brought the burger platters and the conversation slowed down, not much though; we are both good at talking around a mouthful of food.

"I still have to explain *story*." Both his hands full of big burger. "Stories are really powerful. Even God is a story. The Bible says, 'In the beginning was the word and the word was with God and the word was God.' Now, I'm not saying that God is just a story. I'm trying to emphasize how powerful story is."

"Doesn't get you anywhere. Neither you nor I am Christian."

He had a big smile on his face. "Yes, we are."

"Are not."

"Are too."

"Bullshit." I felt a little short on words. But it was a good word that fit the moment.

"We're Christian because we are caught in the Christian story. It's all around us. Remember the big bang?"

I didn't answer. No need, he was going to tell me anyway.

"The reason science adopted a big bang theory is because the first words in the Bible are 'In the beginning.' There really was no big bang."

"So, now you're trying to tell me the universe isn't expanding."

"Oh, it's expanding all right. It just isn't getting any bigger."

"I think I once paid you a hundred dollars because you proved the universe was getting bigger."

He shrugged. "Oh well. You have to pay for your education."

He was right. Oh well. What was a hundred dollars spent years ago? But he wasn't going to get a free lunch out of me now as easily as he had then.

"The reason the universe is expanding and not getting any larger is because it is surrounded by a void. Anything that goes into the void disappears because it has no position. So our universe is constantly being eaten. Same as I explained to you about black holes and gravity. Think of our universe surrounded by a black hole that we are constantly falling into."

No, no, no . . . this wasn't making any sense whatsoever. "If we're surrounded by a black hole, then it's going to eat us up and we'll disappear."

"Except we're growing at the same rate we're being eaten."

I just shook my head. This still wasn't making sense.

"Let me explain." He took an elastic from one of the braids in his beard. "Remember $E=mc^2$?"

I nodded, mouth full of burger.

"Well, all that means is energy equals mass. If I take this elastic and weigh it, I know its mass. If I stretch it" — he pulled on it to show me — "I put energy into it. If I weigh it again while it's stretched, that energy I put into it will increase its mass and it will weigh more."

I had no way to prove or disprove what he was telling me. I had to accept it. "So?"

"So the same thing is happening to the universe. It is being pulled in all directions. It is constantly being stretched, and that stretching is putting energy into it, and that energy is turning into mass, because, like I said, mass and energy are the same thing.

"You remember those little toys we used to play with: tops?"

"Yeah."

He was putting the elastic back on the beard braid.

"Well, if you spin it, put energy into it, it will weigh more than it does while it's stopped. $E=mc^2$ again. The earth is rotating on its axis, same as that top. It has energy that becomes mass, and the earth weighs more because it's spinning than it would if it was stationary."

"So?"

"So the earth is orbiting the sun, and the sun is part of a galaxy orbiting a black hole, and while that black hole at the galaxy's centre is eating the galaxy, at the same time it is causing a whirlpool in space, putting energy into it, creating more mass. The two forces balance each other out. The universe is being eaten by the void that surrounds it, which is stretching it in all directions and creating more mass. And the black holes in the centre of each of the billions of galaxies are creating whirlpool energies that turn into mass. The universe is in a constant state of being created and destroyed at the same time.

"There was no beginning. There doesn't have to be a beginning. We end up thinking there was a beginning only because of the power of the Christian story."

"Two things," I interrupted him. "First is, if I remember right, you once told me the universe began with a spore that spontaneously began to grow. And the second is I still don't get how the planets are formed by energy alone."

"Well, first things first. About that spore, I might have been wrong about that. But if we look at maps of dark matter in the universe, it looks like mycelia. It looks like a web. Back then I still believed the dominant story, which was the big bang story. Now I'm not so sure.

"Your second question is easier. Everything in the universe is made out of space. Remember space is made out of waves. So is everything else. Light can be a photon or a wave. Atoms can be solid or a wave. Physical matter is mostly space." He tapped the table with his knuckle. "This is 95 percent space. The atoms in here are only a small part of it and even the atoms are just a different form of space.

"Remember I explained to you that gravity is just the difference between the low density of space close to the surface of the earth and higher density space farther up?"

I had a solid memory of that.

"Well, it's all about density. At one density space is that stuff out there that keeps the universe together; at another density it becomes dark matter, which is the same stuff that is between the atoms in this table; and at extreme densities it becomes the quarks that make up photons and neutrons and even electrons.

"So while the universe is being stretched and spun by the difference between space and a void, energy is being created, which becomes mass, which becomes stars and planets and galaxies. It's really quite simple. I call it the *Constant State Universe Theory*."

It took a moment to absorb what he'd said. A few mouthfuls of burger. I didn't have any arguments, and anyway that wasn't what we had been talking about. "Okay. I'll accept that maybe the big bang is just a story that came about because of the Christian Genesis story. But how does that make me a racist?"

"Because everything is story: you, me, the universe, everything. Let's try medicine. You know *placebo*."

I nod, my mouth too full to speak. I know placebo.

He explains it anyway. "I give you a sugar pill and tell you a story about how this pill is medicine, and you take it and believe the story, 35 to 50 percent of the time you will experience a reduction in your symptoms. There was a woman who was told she had cancer. She went home and for the next few months she did nothing but watch happy movies. Any movie as long as it had a happy ending. One after the other, anything to take her mind off her cancer. When she went back to the doctor months later, her cancer was gone. There was also a boy with leukemia, imagined that the Lone Ranger was riding through his blood veins, shooting the cancer cells with silver bullets. Guess what, he healed himself. Stories can heal you.

"There's also *nocebo*. If I give you the same sugar pill, but this time I change the story and tell you that it is poison, and if you take the pill and believe the story, you are going to get very sick and maybe even die. There was a guy who tried to commit suicide by taking nocebo pills. His heart rate went down, his blood pressure went down, and he required medical intervention. He didn't begin to recover until they told him the pills he had taken were made out of sugar. It's not the sugar in the pill that does it. It's the story. A story can heal you and a story can kill you."

Either I had nothing to say in response or I was too busy eating.

"Do you remember the shortest story ever written?"

I did. We'd talked about this before. Augusto Monterroso, "When he awoke, the dinosaur was still there."

"Eight words, and the reason it makes sense and can be called a story is because we infer meaning to those words. Who was *he*? A man, a boy, another dinosaur? Was the dinosaur there before he went to sleep or was it in his dreams? Know what I think?"

I shook my head.

"I think there are even shorter stories. I think one word can be a story because we infer meaning into it. Take the word *blasphemy*. We infer a whole volume of ideas into it: witch burnings, crusades, wars, trials, torture, inquisitions. That one word evokes a lot more than its three syllables would suggest. Take the word *adultery*. How many stories can you infer from that word?

"Each word is a story. It is either a placebo or a nocebo story. So we have to be careful with each word that we speak, because, depending on which word we choose, we can either heal or kill.

"I know I'm going a little off topic here..." He put his burger down and wiped the grease from his fingers with a napkin. "If we infer meaning into words and we think with words — well, most of us think with words; some people think with pictures — but if you're one of the majority and your mind is constantly filled with internal dialogue, then maybe we can change our thinking if we change our words.

"If we want to get out of a street gang lifestyle and we're still saying things like 'bro' or 'homey,' our thinking won't change. Or like you with your hard-rock miner, logger, sailor language where you use 'fuck' or 'fucken' in every sentence. If you want to change your thinking, change the words you use."

"Fuck that. I like who I am. And my thinking is perfectly okay with me."

"Up to you, but if you ever want to become something other than working class, change your language. Change the words you talk to yourself with."

"Still haven't fucken proved I'm a racist."

"I'm getting there. I just need you to know that everything is story and that you are the story that you tell yourself."

"Get on with it, then." I deliberately didn't say, *Fuck, get on with it already.*

"I'm going to take my time. Still have a few things

to prove first. You think you see me? You believe what your eyes are telling you?"

"Yeah." I have twenty-twenty vision, maybe even better. I do an exercise when I am on the plane flying in and out of the mine. I read the newspaper of the guy sitting two rows in front of me. Headlines are easy. If I really focus, I can read the regular print as well.

"Impossible. You have two eyes. So you should see two pictures. Each of those pictures should be clearer toward the centre and fuzzy around the periphery because the cones and rods, those things in your eyes that do the actual seeing, are more concentrated closer to the centre. And each of those pictures should have a big black hole in the middle because you can't see through the optic nerve that runs through the centre of your retina. What happens is"—he holds both hands up, palms toward me—"your brain takes these two pictures and merges them together"—he shows me with his hands—"and it fills in the blank spot. Guess what it fills the blank spot in with?"

I shrug.

"Shit you made up."

I don't say anything. He gets tired of waiting for me to respond.

"I'm serious. A lot of what you think you see is socially derived. You are seeing things based upon the story you are living. That's how magicians do their tricks. They can turn a piece of rope into a snake and your eyes actually see the snake. The trick wouldn't work on someone from the High Arctic who had never seen a snake. His brain wouldn't fill in the gap with an image of something that wasn't already stored away."

I wasn't buying it, not completely, not yet.

"You're a writer. Ever edit your own stuff?"

I nod.

"You know why you have such a hard time of it? Because when you are rereading something you wrote, if you made a mistake, if you accidentally wrote *on* instead of *an*, when you reread it, your brain would show you the letter *a* instead of the letter *o*."

"Okay. That's a little more convincing. But I'm still not a racist."

"Do you accept that everything is story, that you and I and the universe are just stories we make up?"

I had to think about it. Did I really accept it? I didn't feel like a story. I felt real. But I had no way to prove I was real. And that thing about not knowing anything because everything we think we know is inferred based on things we inferred earlier—that I couldn't argue with. "Okay, I buy it. But if I am nothing more than the stories I tell myself, then I am in control and I choose not to be a racist."

"You are in control." He finished his hamburger and began working on the pile of fries, one at a time. "You can change it, but you have to know what it is first; you have to know the story."

"So tell me. What do you think the story is?"

He waited, a fry between thumb and forefinger. "There are all sorts of stories that we never challenge. Canada is just a story. We made it up. We say we are kinder, gentler Americans. We could have said anything. The constitution is just a story. We wrote it. We could have written it any other way. The worst thing about the nation story is that people believe it and are willing to die for it. We go to war and kill other people because of the story we tell ourselves.

"That company you work for, Cameco—it's just a story. The only reason Cameco has any power is because we all agree it has power. It's the story we tell about it. If everyone agrees on the story, it doesn't matter that the only real essence of the company is a charter and a set of bylaws filed away at Corporations Branch. Cameco has no body to kick, no soul to damn. The only place it exists is in our heads."

"Yeah, but that story writes me a very real pay-cheque every two weeks."

"How real is that paycheque?"

"I say it's real. It buys me a lot of stuff, and as of now I still don't think it's going to buy lunch."

"That cheque is like money. They're both made out of paper. Take any bill out of your wallet, hold it in your hand, and you see a piece of paper with a picture of either an old woman or some dead guy on it. Tilley is going to take that piece of paper in exchange for this meal because she believes the story about money. The only reason money works is because everyone believes the fiction. It's okay. We all get along and things get done. We build roads and hospitals and schools and pay the workers with paper, and everyone agrees and everyone is happy with it."

He finished his last fry and was looking around to see where Tilley might be. "The problem with the money fiction is at a higher level: the economy. We used to believe in dragons and unicorns; now we believe in market forces. This new story demands human sacrifice. There are people on this planet who are starving to death, and we have way too much food here."

I look at his gravy-smeared plate and at mine, which still holds a few vinegar-soaked fries and a bit of coleslaw.

"But if we took some of our food and gave it to them, the economy would suffer. So, to keep the economy story going, some people have to die. Nobody questions the story. It's taken as natural and normal and even necessary. That's the thing. These stories we make up take off on us and we lose control. Pretty soon we accept the story as reality.

"Our brains believe the story that we never question, and when we see things, the brain fills in the empty spots with those stories. Remember that woman who asked you for money on the way here?"

I remembered. Gave her a few quarters.

"What you thought you saw wasn't what was there."

"So what was there, then? She certainly was no princess."

"No, she wasn't a princess. But she wasn't what you saw either. What your eyes told you was based upon that lazy dirty drunken Indian story."

"Fuck off." I could see where this was going and I didn't like it.

"She wasn't as dirty or drunk as your eyes told you she was."

"Bullshit, she was drunk. I could smell it on her."

"She had a little buzz going. If she had been a white male, you wouldn't have minded as much. That lazy dirty drunken Indian story is so powerful, it has been around for so long, and we've been hearing it since first contact, throughout the colonial period, again in residential schools, and we are still hearing it in the media. Oh, they've toned it down some, but it's still there. Not only have we heard it again and again, we repeat it again and again. It's in the jokes we tell: 'How do you hide something from an Indian? Put it in his work boots.' You know how it goes."

"Bullshit!" I knew I was repeating myself. It was just that what he was saying was beginning to hit a little too close to home. "Remember I'm half Indian."

"That just makes it worse. We take those stories about ourselves and internalize them. Indians hate Indians too. Why do you think there is so much violence in our communities? Indians beat up Indians because the guy, or even the woman, they are beating on is an Indian. It's very rare for an Indian to assault a white person. It might happen, but not often. And the worst part is, why do Indian men beat up Indian women? Because they're women. In that story about how much lesser we are, the lowest of the low is the woman.

"Admit it. When you were single, you preferred to be with Indian women because the story was that they were easy."

"That's not what I said. If I remember right, I once told you that I found Indian women were not as uptight as white women about sex."

"Same thing. Just a different way of saying it."

This was getting too hard to accept. "Keep in mind, our mother is an Indian woman."

"That's how powerful the story is. You were raised by a brown-skinned woman who loved you, and you still treated that woman on Central Avenue like she was something lesser."

"I gave her money," I defended.

"You gave her a bit of change to get rid of her. Your eyes told you she was drunk and dirty, and you didn't want to be around her."

I was glad Tilley came over right then to clean away our platters and take our pie orders: raisin and ice cream for Clifford, apple and ice cream for me. While we waited, I was able to let everything he said settle. I was able to let all the things I was feeling settle. My first response had been a rush of anger, and I knew enough not to say anything until it subsided. We ate mostly in silence. Tilley cuts her pies into sixths rather than eighths and she piles on the ice cream.

Later, sipping coffee, feeling content, Clifford continued: "You know, it's not just the racism we feel toward others. And, yeah, I am caught in it too. I have to be extra careful to make sure that my eyes are seeing what's actually in front of me. And it's not just our eyes. Our brain hears what it wants to hear. It interprets the sounds we hear and will change words around on us."

That was easier to accept than the idea that our eyes lie to us. I could easily remember a dozen times when I heard something wrongly. Always wrote it off as being because I worked around too many chainsaws and diesel engines.

"All those stories about us being 'lesser than' because we're half-breeds get inside our heads and we believe them. The reason you quit the navy and came home is because they offered you advance promotion and officer training. Your brain told you that you weren't able to do that, you were just a half-breed and couldn't be an officer."

"I quit the navy because I was done with it and I was drinking too much there."

"You drank the same amount when you got home. And what about that promotion at the mine that you purposely fucked up?"

The foreman, Chuck Gastell, had told me that he was planning on having me act as relief foreman when he took his holidays. I came back to him a few hours later and told him that I needed help dealing with my overuse of marijuana. When I had told Clifford about it, I was wondering why it seemed like I had purposely sabotaged myself. He didn't have an answer then. He had one now. And I didn't like it.

In the end I paid for the meal. Not because he had proven that I was a racist. I still had trouble accepting that. I paid because I couldn't prove that I wasn't.

I AM STORY, Dad was story. Clifford...

The night is very late, the darkest part of the dark and the coldest. I lie back down and pull up the sleeping bag. The earth beneath me is comforting, warm and soft. I feel cuddled by the tree roots on either side. The air is absolutely still. The only sound is of my own breathing, my own heartbeat. If Clifford was right, that I am just the story that I tell myself...

But he's wrong. Isn't he? I am also all the stories he told me. And why did he tell me all those stories? What was he trying to make me into?

I can smell the pine needles mixed with the scent of soil. I feel the tension draining away, and sleep draws me into the darkness. Just before I fall away, my arm reaches out, my hand finds the hoop, and I bring it close. I realize that I have done it without thinking, that my arm and my hand seem to have acted of their own accord. I'm too tired to think about it anymore, and anyway, it feels right.

PARALLEL TRUTHS

I AM NOT FINISHED.

I awaken in the darkest part of the night and know that I am not going to get away that easily. There is still something that needs to be done; something I should have taken care of a long time ago. I had fallen asleep thinking I had reconciled everything. I was wrong.

No sense lying here. I am not going to sleep.

I get up. The fire has burned down and there are only coals remaining. I stir them with a long stick and add two small pieces of wood that I had cut and set aside. They smoulder. They'll take a minute before they light.

The stars tell me it's about 3:00 a.m., maybe 3:30.

The night is silent: no birds, no squirrels, not even mice scurrying in the dry pine needles. The air is still and feels thick. I stand, listening intently. It's as though the darkness has smothered any sound. All I hear is my own slow breathing and my heartbeat, and even they are muted.

I need to apologize.

Or do I?

He knew.

Knew all along.

He knew before I told him.

We had been at Mom's house, probably both of us home at the same time, maybe it was Christmas. I don't remember. I do remember the kitchen table, chrome and plastic-covered chairs, and as always a cup of coffee in front of each of us.

I was telling him about a fight. Our nephew Paulie and I, in a truck, drunk, driving across the prairie in the night at the end of some celebration. Clarence had been in the middle. I was driving and Paul had the passenger side. Paulie was being an asshole. He pulled the truck out of gear. Just reached over in front of Clarence and knocked the shifter into neutral. For no good reason other than we were all drunk and he was trying to annoy me. It worked. I put the truck back into gear and told him to smarten the fuck up. He didn't wait very long before he did it again. Maybe he thought it was funny.

I didn't.

This time when I put the truck back into gear, I reached across and backhanded him across the face. "Fuck around some more, asshole." Then we were fighting. I was driving with one hand. Clarence was dodging fists coming from both sides as Paulie and I punched at each other. I hit the brakes hard. Skidded the truck sideways down the road and off into some farmer's field. Paulie was going to fucken get it this time. I'd had enough of him.

As soon as the truck stopped, I was out the door and coming around to his side to get him. In any fight speed matters. The quickest way to the passenger side was through the box of the truck. I jumped over the side, was halfway across when I saw the shovel.

Paulie and Donny, our youngest brother, are the same age, only a few days between their birthdays. He and Paul have had many fist fights. I should have listened to Donny. He said, "Don't ever waste your time hitting that fucker in the head. It doesn't do any good. May as well punch a rock."

When Paulie came out that passenger door, I hit

him with the shovel, over the head. There was good steel in that spade. The *ding* it made sounded like a bell. I hit him again, harder. *DING.*

And the fucker didn't go down.

Now I was in trouble. He was four inches taller with longer arms and he had forty pounds on me.

I dropped the useless shovel and grabbed him by the Adam's apple and squeezed hard. That didn't work either. He just grabbed me by the throat the same way.

The fight ended in a draw, with both of us standing in the middle of the road, squeezing each other's Adam's apples, both of us enduring the pain but refusing to give up.

When we dropped Paulie off outside his apartment in Saskatoon, the last thing he said was, "Fuck, Uncle, I can't believe you hit me with a shovel."

Clifford and I are sitting at Mom's kitchen table and I am telling him about the fight. "I don't know, there's something about Paulie. He's never done me any wrong. I have no reason to be pissed at him, but somehow he always manages to piss me off. It's like I'm permanently annoyed with him."

Clifford doesn't say anything.

I keep talking, probably repeating myself. "I don't

know why I'm so pissed at him all the time. He tries to be a good guy around me, always anxious to lend a hand. I know if I ask him, he'll rush right over and help me out with whatever I need help with. But it's like I'm permanently upset with him, and it's not his fault."

Clifford looks up, looks directly at me. His voice is soft yet serious. "Maybe you did something to him that you can't forgive yourself for."

All of a sudden we are not talking about Paulie anymore.

We're talking about us.

"You knew?" I ask.

"I've always known," he says as he gets up, walks over, and puts his cup in the sink.

My mind is numb. I feel an old hurt welling up: regret, guilt, and shame.

As he walks by, he drops his left hand on my left shoulder. I can feel it now, standing in the dark, in the silence of the middle of the night. "It's okay," he says. Makes a joke of it to ease my hurt: "Mom told us that brothers are supposed to share."

The darkness feels even thicker now, suffocating.

The two sticks in the coals are beginning to smoulder, I can smell the smoke. I feel a sting start behind my eyes, a tightness in my throat, an ache in my core that catches my breath. I turn my back away from the smoke and look out into the black of the forest and speak, softly at first, then with more purpose: "I'm sorry. I am sorry. It should never have happened. I have no reason and no excuse."

The night doesn't answer.

"I didn't mean to fuck your wife."

It still doesn't answer.

I HAD BEEN in a relationship with a woman from up north that didn't work out. I was too young to be in a relationship, didn't know how relationships worked. I found my way to Clifford's at about five in the morning, parked my car behind his house, and let myself in the back door. His wife came downstairs to meet me. Clifford stayed in bed. He had to get up later and go to work.

I was telling her what my broken heart felt like. We were sitting on the couch, sharing a joint that she had saved for a special occasion, and she leaned over and kissed me, on the mouth.

I kissed her back.

She got up, took me by the hand, and led me to the spare downstairs bedroom. And we fucked.

And I never forgave myself for it.

A year later. They had moved. Clifford had taken a job in a mining camp, finally making some decent money, but it meant that he had to be away from home for weeks at a time. His wife asked Mom to babysit while she went uptown.

Mom said, "The bitch probably threw a packsack over the fence before she left, because she never did come home."

And I knew it was my fault. Maybe not entirely, but I had contributed to the breakdown of my brother's marriage. I was to blame.

From then on, I had treated him like a bastard.

Not all the time, but enough.

There was a distance and a strain between us that I was never able to reconcile. It made me challenge him more often. And I put him down. It wasn't brothers being tough with each other, that was some of it; there was also an undercurrent of my simply being mean to him.

He'd asked to borrow a few dollars, needed groceries. I gave him a fifty, knowing I'd never see it again. I pulled out my full wallet, plucked a pink bill from the fold, and handed it to him. As he took it, I said, "Get a fucken job, bum."

It could have been a joke, just brotherly bantering, one-upping, verbal rowdiness, but it wasn't. It was mean and we both knew it. He needed money to feed his kids. I had lots. And I chose to be an asshole about it.

"I'm sorry," I say again to the dark. "Clifford, I am so fucken sorry." The snot is beginning to flow and the sting behind my eyes cools itself with a release of tears. The ache in my core swallows my heart and my lungs, and I am so empty inside that my shoulders slump and my spine weakens and curls until I am bowed with my head down. My grief isn't finished with me yet. It feels all raw and bloody and fresh.

"I'm sorry."

I don't have anything else to say, and now that he is gone, it seems like a waste of words. If I'd only said it sooner, when it still might have meant something.

I feel his presence. More than just the sensation of his hand on my shoulder a minute ago. It's like he's out there, not far, in the darkness, close enough to hear. I say it again. This time speaking directly to him. "I am sorry. How do I make it right?"

I hear the answer. I don't know if I hear it with my ears, if the words pierced the silence, or if I hear it in my head or maybe I might have spoken. I doubt it was me because the words are in his voice. There are only two words: *parallel truths*.

There is one more sound: a sniffle as I stop crying, wipe my eyes with my sleeve. I get it. There is no single answer. All answers are equally true.

WE HAD BEEN travelling. We were either going south, or back up north on that stretch of pavement between Prince Albert and La Ronge. I don't remember direction. I only remember boreal. The forest on both sides of the road, and I am driving and as usual I am driving fast. It's not that I particularly like speed. It's in everything I do. I am a logger, miner, sailor man, and I do everything flat out.

Damn the torpedoes; full speed ahead.

I am young and full of testosterone and I can outwork any man, day or night. I don't take any shit and I say it the way I see it.

"You know all that stuff about space being something and gravity and black holes is all just a big crock of shit, don't you?"

I'm starting a conversation because there is no radio reception unless we want to listen to the CBC and I am starting the conversation on my terms.

He's quiet. Sitting and thinking and hasn't said a word in the last fifty miles.

"Really," I continue. "If you are right about all that stuff, then every scientist on the planet has to be wrong. Space is a field. It's not made of waves and it isn't space that gives matter substance. It's the Higgs boson."

He's quiet, maybe getting his mind into place, letting things settle.

I wait.

He looks out at the passing forest.

He is silent for so long that I begin to think he might not answer. Maybe he's just ignoring me. I am about to take another verbal shot at him to stir him up when he finally turns back to me and says, "You know about workers' compensation, don't you?"

"What the fuck are you talking about?"

"Workers' comp. You're a union guy. You know about workers' compensation."

"What's that got to do with anything?"

"It's the same. You know that when a worker gets hurt on the job, he can't sue the employer; he has to go to workers' comp. To most people workers' comp is a good thing. Means the worker doesn't have to hire a lawyer, doesn't have to go to court and maybe lose. It's a good deal, right?"

"Yeah, workers' comp is a good deal. But what's that got to do with anything?" I ask again.

"Well, there's the other truth. Workers' comp injures workers."

"Where's your proof?"

He smiles. "It comes from you. Remember telling me about the guy who tried to cut through his safety pads with a chainsaw because he was sure that if he did he would get compensation?"

I remembered. I wasn't there when it happened. Just a story that went around the logging camps, how the guy had revved up his saw until it was screaming and slammed it down into the safety pad on his leg, but the saw didn't cut through; it kicked back and caught him in the face.

Clifford didn't have to remind me of the other guy working in a fence post–cutting camp who held up a fence post with one hand and, using an axe, deliberately chopped off his thumb.

"And it's not just the ones who do it deliberately," he continues. "It's also that workers' comp makes people careless. It doesn't matter if they get hurt because they're covered.

"Two truths. Workers' comp is a good thing. Workers' comp is a bad thing. And they are both true at the same time. It's what I call *parallel truths*.

"I've talked to you about this before. Placebo—nocebo. They are both sugar pills. If I give you one and tell you it's medicine and it is good for you, you will probably get better. If I give you the same sugar pill and tell you it's poison, and you take it and believe the story, you are going to get sick and maybe even die. It's the same pill. Placebo and nocebo are the same thing with completely different results. They're parallel stories. Both true at the same time."

"Okay," I reply, "but what's that got to do with your version of science?"

"Science is a story. My story about how the universe works is just as true as the dominant story. They're parallel truths, both true at the same time."

"Two things can't be true at the same time. It's either one or the other," I argue back.

"That's pretty shallow thinking. Deterministic. You can do better than that. You have a mind that is capable of simultaneous thought at a multitude of levels. You just have to let it do what it is able to do."

I had to watch the road, especially at the speed I was driving, so I couldn't look at his face to read what was behind the words. The tone told me he was being serious, that he was in his teaching mode.

"There are all kinds of parallel truths," he continued. "You, for example. You're an asshole and a good guy. You take pride in your tough-guy, hard-ass way of being. And at the same time you can be very kind to people."

"Only people who don't piss me off." I must have been upholding the tough guy he was threatening with his talk of kindness.

He ignored me. "Parallel truths are everywhere. You're one."

He let the words hang there for a moment. Let them sink in before continuing.

"I recognize that I am multiple truths and don't confine myself to one way of thinking. It makes it easier to manoeuvre because I am not confined to a single thought pattern."

What he is saying strikes me as being wishy-washy. "You're just taking the easy way out so you don't have to take a position and defend it."

"It's actually harder to defend multiple truths because most people are programmed to believe there is only one absolute truth. That's the problem." He is facing away from me, watching the trees zip past on the side of the highway. "Most of the wars are about interpretation and belief in absolute single truths. Catholicism and Protestantism are parallel stories of the same Christian story, but try to tell that to the Irish who kill each other because each believes their version of the story is true.

"Christianity and Islam and Judaism are all parallel stories. Remember Isaac and Ishmael were brothers."

"Who?" I don't know this story.

"Isaac and Ishmael." He pauses. "Old Testament. Abraham and Sarah were too old to have children and Sarah told him to take the maid. He did and his first son was Ishmael. Then he knocked up Sarah and their kid was Isaac. Then Sarah got jealous of Ishmael and had Abraham send him and his mother away. The story goes that God promised Ishmael that he would found a great nation and that Isaac would continue Abraham's line. That's how we end up with Arabs and Jews. They are the same story. Parallel stories."

Either I hadn't heard that one before, or I hadn't heard it in a long time. I let it sink in, with all the ramifications — the Middle East conflict, crusades, oil...

A few thoughts later he says, "Capitalism and socialism are the same industrial stories, and they both have the same purpose: to get workers into the factories. The socialist tells the people that everyone deserves a job and that labour unions are there for their protection. The capitalist tells the people that they have to work hard and lift themselves up by their bootstraps. But it's the same story. They both want workers to move to the city and work in their factories. Socialism and capitalism are different sides of the same industrial coin. They are the new religions, and they are parallel stories.

"You're a trade unionist?"

I look over at him. He is turned in his seat, facing me. It's a question. So I answer it. "Damn right."

"Labour and management are parallel stories. What you do to one, you do to the other. If you go on strike, you hurt management—but you hurt yourself at the same time. Together the two stories merge and make the story of the corporation.

"You know about entangled particles?"

I sort of did, but... "You're jumping all over the place here. One thing at a time. I can see how parallel stories work with religions that have the same roots with a monotheistic god and that each believes they alone know the one truth. I can even accept that workers and bosses need each other, but science... Shouldn't that at least be a consistent story?"

"Consistency doesn't need to be singular." He's smiling. "Entangled particles. Remember what Einstein called 'spooky action at a distance.'"

I remembered. Cause two particles to become entangled and then separate them, and what you did to one immediately caused the other one to react, and the reaction happened faster than the speed of light. "So now you are going to tell me that the particles are stories," I guessed.

"Sort of." He paused. "I had thought that for a while. No, the particles are not stories but they are parallel. It's a good analogy of parallel stories but it doesn't quite capture it. I just figured out what is going on there before you interrupted my thoughts with your questions. Here's what I think. Remember how I was telling you that the universe is expanding because it is surrounded by a void and the void is stretching it and by stretching it, it's putting energy into the universe, and when you have enough energy, it becomes matter?"

He was completely changing the subject. But, yes, I remembered.

"Well, it doesn't quite work out. The stretching alone can't account for all the energy. It takes a lot of energy to become matter. $E=mc^2$ means that you have to move mass at the square of the speed of light before it becomes energy. Say it the other way, and you need energy equal to the square of the speed of light to make matter. It's too much. One spoon of sugar contains enough energy to flatten a city the size of New York. That's where the idea of the atom bomb came from.

"If all matter used to be energy, there's too much matter in the universe. There couldn't be that much original energy. So what I think is going on is those entangled particles are actually the same particle in two places at the same time."

"Whoa, whoa," I interrupt. The ramifications are too big. If every particle in the universe was entangled with another particle somewhere else in the universe and they were the same particle, then the universe has only half the mass we think it has. "Things can't be in two places at the same time."

"Sure they can, if we introduce the idea of a void. Remember that in a pure void an object would be everywhere and nowhere at the same time."

"But that's only in the void that surrounds the universe and in black holes. The universe is not a void." I ease off on the gas pedal. I can't drive fast and think all this through at the same time.

Clifford's voice shows his excitement. He obviously just figured this out while we were talking. It's as fresh to him as it is to me. "If the only voids are black holes and the one that surrounds the universe; but what if each atom was a quasi-void?"

"Quasi-void?" I ask. "Wouldn't it be a void or no void? Something or nothing?"

"No, what we are dealing with is space. That's the thing. That's the magic. Space does all the work. Through it, energy becomes matter and things have position. But if space is a wave, like I think, then when we change its frequency it becomes something else, like light or gamma rays or whatever. Whenever we put energy into space, space changes. So what's going on inside the atom?"

I know the answer. "Positively charged proton, neutrally charged neutron combined in a nucleus, and negatively charged electrons in orbit around the nucleus."

"Wrong," he replies. "That's what they taught you at the mines when they were trying to explain nuclear radiation. It's a simple way of looking at the atom so that you can say alpha radiation is caused by neutrons, and beta radiation is caused by protons, and gamma radiation is pure energy from the nucleus.

But that's not how it really works. The proton and neutron do make up the core of the atom, but the electron is not in orbit like a planet around the sun. The uncertainty principle says that the electron is everywhere and nowhere around the nucleus at the same time. You can know its location or its velocity but never both at the same time. I think the reason is because of the incredible amount of energy in the atom. Square the speed of light to give the proton and neutron mass. All that energy has displaced space. Remember you need space to have place. So where the electron exists is in the quasi-void where space has been pushed back by the atom's energy.

"And if I am right about this, then every atom has a tiny void in it, and because position can't exist in a void, a particle can be in two places at the same time. And not just two places. There's no reason why it couldn't be in multiple places at the same time.

"Hey, you know what. If voids can exist at the core of an atom, there is no reason they can't be everywhere." He is obviously thinking this up as he's speaking. It comes through in his eagerness. "Sure, that would explain the particle-antiparticle problem. There should be as many antiparticles as there are particles in the universe. It's baffled science as to what happened to them. Voids explain where they went."

"Hold on, hold on. Where are all these voids? Are you talking about black holes?"

"No," he answers. "Space doesn't have to be continuous. If there were tiny voids throughout it, we wouldn't notice. They would be undetectable to us because they are nothing. There is no reason why half the space between you and I"—he waves his hand in the air to show me the space between us—"isn't made up of little voids that we can't perceive.

"Yeah, this makes sense. The difference between a particle and an antiparticle is simply that particles exist in space and the unique properties of antiparticles only allows them to exist in voids."

He leans back and thinks about what he just said. A thin smile shows. A moment later he says: "Imagine . . . Somewhere else in the universe you and I are driving along, having this same conversation. We are there and here at the same time and it doesn't matter."

And now he is somewhere else in the universe and I am here. Maybe we were parallel stories. What I did to him, he did to me. Even if we were not parallel stories, we were entangled particles. There is no asking Clifford for a solution to the riddle. It's too late for that. Any chance at an explanation ended with a knock on the door.

TWO HOURS

SEPTEMBER 1, 1985, at about nine o'clock in the morning. I never saw it coming.

Night shift was over. Abe Weins and I were playing backgammon, smoking a bit of homegrown, and drinking homemade crabapple wine. We had been friends for a long time. We were both heavy-equipment operators for Cameco Corporation at the Key Lake Uranium Mine. I mostly drove a truck, hauling waste or ore out of the open pit, sometimes on a dozer or grader or loader or something to break up the monotony of mining production. The work was one week of twelve-hour shifts at the mine and then one week at home. It was a civilized rotation. Before working for this company I had put in many three-week shifts followed by one week off. I had also worked five-, seven-, and eleven-week rotations. Week in/week out was almost a holiday.

Backgammon: a dollar a game and the doubling cube; we kept a score sheet and paid up at the end of the week. Some weeks he owed me twenty bucks; another week and I owed him twenty. Backgammon is a game of chance.

Abe grew the marijuana on his farm. He liked to say, "Pure organic, nothing added to it other than a bit of pig shit." He also made the wine, was proud of his brewing skills and his Mennonite upbringing that didn't allow him to spend a penny that didn't need to be spent.

We played in my room because I had a better sound system. We were listening to either Huey Lewis and the News or Mark Knopfler and Dire Straits. Kept the volume down, kept our voices down, some people go straight to bed after night shift. We preferred to party a bit, go to sleep a little later so that we woke up just before we had to go back to work.

We were upstairs in E wing of a three-hundred-man modern camp that was quite luxurious. Someone had nicknamed it Hotel California; you can check out but you can never leave. We were laughing and throwing dice when the recreational director knocked on the door.

He'd been sent upstairs by Garnet Wipf from Personnel.

When I got downstairs, Garnet explained: "I didn't want to come up on my own, never know what you might have been doing up there, whether you had a bottle or not." It was understood. If Garnet caught me with a bottle, he would have to take disciplinary action and I could be fired. Everyone knew that Garnet Wipf would fire you. He was the most hated man who ever walked. You'd wait a long time to hear a good word about him at the Key Lake site. Up until that day I'd had no contact with him, had no judgement of him.

"What's up?" I hoped I wasn't slurring my words, hoped my eyes weren't too bloodshot, not too glazed.

"Bad news. We got a call from the RCMP in Pine House. They want you to give them a call."

"Did they say what it's about?"

"No, just that it was very important and they want you to give them a call."

The phones in the camp didn't work. The Key Lake mine site was about 125 miles north of the nearest community, the village of Pine House, which was itself already remote. Phone service that far from the settled South of the province was at best sporadic.

"It's okay, you can use the phone at Administration. We're on a different line from the camp's," Garnet offered.

The administration building was over with the mill operations, about a mile from the camp. I phoned the RCMP in Pine House from Garnet's office. He shut the door for privacy.

"Hello. This is Ray Johnson up at the Key Lake site. You guys wanted me to give you a call."

"Yes, Ray. We have a message from the Prince Albert detachment. Someone in your family has died."

"Who?"

"I'm not sure, and I'm not going to say until I am sure. Please stay where you are and I will call you back when I know."

Then the negotiations began.

Someone in my family —

I had two children, Michael and Harmony. Mike was eight; Harmony, four. We lived in the little town of Saint Louis beside the South Saskatchewan River. It was a fast-flowing river . . .

There was a street in front of the house. There was

traffic on that street. Mike and Harmony sometimes played on that street...

Please God. Not my children.

It was a gravel street.

Mom lived across that street. She'd come to visit after we bought our house there. She liked the community, and we helped her to get into a low-rent apartment for seniors right across the street. I couldn't get the image of that strip of gravel bounded by sidewalks out of my head. Mom's health wasn't that good, and she liked to walk down to the pub on an afternoon...

Please God. Not my mom.

My brothers Garry and Donny had been planning a hunting trip up the Bow River...

Oh God. No, not my brothers. Please.

Clarence was working, driving truck...

Jimmy was mining...

Richard was mining...

Stanley was working for a crane company...

Possibilities.

Industrial possibilities.

Industrial probabilities...

Shelly, my wife.

Our marriage wasn't going so well.

I married her because I got her pregnant and it was the right thing to do, the honourable thing. But I did love her. I really did. We stayed together for more than just the sake of the children.

But her sister had committed suicide and Shelly wasn't happy…

Who?

Someone in my family.

Who?

It was two hours from the knock on the door until the return phone call from the Pine House RCMP. The negotiations had been intense.

God is a bastard to negotiate with.

He had me cornered, nailed down. I'd fought hard, battled with him, all of my determination and will, and in the end…

In the end I'd traded them all, every one of them: Mom — my brothers — Shelly — every one of them, for my children.

Please God, anybody — but not Harmony or Michael.

Two hours.

Two hours from when I found out someone in my family had died — two fucken hours until I learned who in my family had died.

Clifford.

"Oh fuck!"

Clifford was killed in a car accident.

"Fuck. Now what? Fuck." I wanted to shout. I wanted to punch someone, something. "Now what?"

"I've chartered a plane to fly you out. It'll be here in about an hour. Come on, I'll drive you back to camp so that you can pack." Garnet leads, directs. At one point he said, "I'm not trying to boss you around. I know that you're in shock and you're having a hard time making decisions right now. I'll walk you through it. Now you have to go upstairs and pack your things. You're going home. Where do you fly out to?"

"Prince Albert. Yeah, Prince Albert. But my truck's not there. I loaned it to the people I have working for me."

I was such a workaholic that I had been trying to run a fence post–cutting operation on my week out and had a couple of Shelly's cousins working for me.

"Not to worry. My truck is at the Prince Albert airport." Garnet handed me a set of keys. "Just leave it where you found it."

I also didn't have any money. Payday wasn't until Thursday. I hadn't brought any cash to camp with me because I wouldn't need it.

Garnet dug in his wallet. "Here's forty bucks." He handed me two twenties. It was the last he had.

This was from the asshole whom everyone in camp hated.

IT'S A HARD memory to go through. Was it already a week? One whole week since I negotiated with God. Fly out—meet up with my family—all the brothers, now there are only six of us, two sisters, nephews, and nieces. We gather around Mom. She says she has buried her husband, both her parents, brothers, and a sister, but the hardest thing she has ever had to do was bury one of her children.

A drunk driver, they said.

Clifford was on his way to Yorkton to go to school. Finally, he'd found a job, something that he wanted to do. There are several local radio stations across northern Saskatchewan; each little community has its own. He'd scored the position of being the person who maintained them. He just had to go to school for nine months for an upgrade.

It happened at the S curve just north of Prince Albert. He was only a few miles away from the campground where he intended to spend the night.

His three sons were in the truck with him: Clifford, Brian, and Daniel, thirteen, eleven, and nine. The oldest boy, Clifford, is still in an induced coma, his face smashed in. Brian and Daniel weren't physically injured.

Slam!

You're knocked on your ass.

Unprepared.

There's no fixing something like that. You can't go back and make it better.

I didn't get any warnings, no premonitions. A bird didn't fly into my house. A woodpecker didn't come and warn me. Nothing. I was playing backgammon, smoking pot, and drinking homemade crabapple wine. It was a beautiful day, sunshine, the leaves were getting ready to change and I didn't see this coming.

They wouldn't tell me who the other driver was. Mom's instructions, my youngest brother, Donny, and I were not to be told: "I lost one son, I don't want to see any of the others end up in jail over this." When I recognized her rationale, I didn't ask. If I didn't know, I didn't have to do anything about it. It's best that way. And Mom was right. We had enough to take care of.

Six brothers as pallbearers.

But the ceremony of funeral couldn't heal all the hurts.

It happened too fast.

I am as guilty as the rest of them.

My "work hard, fight hard" military attitude had come between Clifford and me. I was as pissed at him as everyone else. What the fuck was he doing? He had three sons to look after and wouldn't get a job, lived on welfare. He was an embarrassment, and we all took turns telling him so or letting him know in other ways that we didn't approve.

Then, when he got a job...

And he was happy again...

And his life had purpose and he was going to do something...

And it was too late to say *sorry*.

Clarence had been the hardest on him, the most outspoken and direct, and when Clifford died, it hit Clarence the hardest. By the time it was over, Clarence had a very good understanding of Clifford's situation. We'd talked yesterday, Clarence and I, about Clifford's depression at his wife's running away and his subsequent inability to maintain employment. I'd never seen Clarence cry before.

It was a hard thing to watch.

FEAR OF DEATH

SORROW PULLS AT ME. It tries to find the empty space.
But I have had enough. I have given my grief all it
needs. I am drained and there is nothing left to drag
out of me. In the days between the phone call and the
burial yesterday, family came together and we held
each other up. My wife, Shelly, held me, the door
to our bedroom closed so the children would not
see while I cried, while I sobbed huge, wet, snotty
sobs, an ache in my throat and a heavy weight in my
chest. The physical manifestations of grief bend the
spine; I could not stand up straight. I could not raise
my head. Grief dragged at my feet until I shuffled. It
robbed food of its flavour, and I ate the sandwiches at
the wake only because I needed their energy.

The first days were a struggle, reeling, unbelieving, even denying, expecting any minute to hear Clifford laughing at this joke that has no punchline. But he doesn't laugh, and the reality of what is going on builds with the view of each relative's tear-stained face. Mom was the most experienced at grief; she had lost her husband, both her parents, her favourite brother, and her little sister. We were standing in front of the church, getting ready to go in, and again she said, "This is the hardest, losing one of your children." Then she took my sister's arm and walked with her, shared her strength.

I stood outside, over and away from the doors, waiting for the hearse to arrive with the coffin with my brother, with the guest of honour, with our reason for being here, loggers and miners dressed in unfamiliar suits and ties.

Six brothers as pallbearers, black ribbons pinned to our sleeves, carry the coffin from the hearse into the church, and as we go through the doors, I wish there was another way of doing this ceremony of offering Clifford to the sky. I have no memory of Clifford's ever walking into a church. He shunned organized religion, preferring rationality and his own ways of knowing. The only way to get him in was to carry him.

Repeatedly in the days between, brothers told brothers, "Clifford would have wanted..." His sons were told, "Your dad would have wanted..." Have a good life, remember the good times. Decisions were made based upon what Clifford would have wanted; all except this—this Christian ceremony of funeral. No one bothered to ask themselves whether he would have wanted this. This is for the people, for the aunts and cousins, for Mom.

He didn't resist. He didn't kick at the casket and refuse.

We took him through the funeral rites of the Anglican Church on the rock beside Lac La Ronge, then we six brothers wearing black put him again in the hearse for the fifty-mile ride back here to Molanosa, to bury him beside Dad in the graveyard where all the other gone relatives have markers over their bones.

I feel an ache at the memory, wriggle deeper into the hollow of the tree roots, pull the sleeping bag tighter around me, not because I am cold, but just for the closeness, for the comfort.

One of our conversations when we were both still single, before we each married and made children and our lives became less entangled with each other and more wrapped up in our own families: I had spoken brazenly, arrogantly even, regurgitated Nietzsche: "God is dead."

"What are you reading?" Clifford reached over and flipped up the cover of the book in my hands. *Thus Spake Zarathustra.* "You be careful with that."

Why should I be careful with it? It was from his bookshelf.

I closed it, set it on my lap. The morning of reading—Clifford in the armchair, myself stretched out on our couch, a few hours of early-day silence broken occasionally as one or the other of us rose to go to the coffee pot, refill a cup, and return nose-first into paper and pages—was over. Now for conversation.

It was a common routine between us. To read, then discuss. We had been here many times before. I waited. I had started the conversation part of the morning, let him answer. Was God dead or not?

He began with something not only uncharacteristic of him, but also something he had insisted was the weakest of all arguments. Instead of confronting Nietzsche's ideas, he attacked the man.

"All of his ideas come from his fear of death."

I waited. There had to be more to come.

But it turned out to be more than a pause in conversation. I waited while Clifford went to the coffee pot. There was a cup of black at the bottom. He picked it up, swirled it, looked through the glass at the colour and thickness of it, put his nose over the rim and smelled, then poured it down the sink and carefully prepared a new pot.

While we waited for a new brew, I rinsed my cup in anticipation, had time to think through the minutes of silence broken only by the burping of the electric coffee maker. Nietzsche said God was dead because he was afraid of his own death. I tried to connect the two concepts, but the connector refused to show itself.

The last drips plopped into the pot. Clifford first removed the lid and stirred because the stronger coffee is always at the bottom and the weaker at the top. It was either an act of fairness that we each got the same strength brew or he didn't want the weak top cup.

Mine black with half a teaspoon of sugar just to cut the bitter; his with milk and a whole spoonful of white refined.

Back on the couch, my feet flat upon the floor, I tasted, a sip, strong, black, earthy, with a hint of sweet, held the cup with two hands, felt the warmth with my fingers.

Clifford back in the armchair, only the heel of his right foot on the floor, his legs outstretched, crossed, relaxed. He tasted his once, then again, before putting the cup aside.

I lost patience. "So why was Nietzsche afraid of death?"

He didn't answer the question directly. Instead, he looked at me, directly into my eyes.

A staring contest?

Maybe.

I never lose these. I stared back into his, into the green and the blue and the grey, that blend that defied description. But it wasn't a competition. He was looking into my soul.

"You know," he began, "you have always known — ever since you came into this world, you have known. There is a truth, an absolute truth, and you have been aware of it all of your life. You have a sense, an understanding that has always been there that tells you *one* thing. That one thing is that you were destined for greatness. It is so much a part of you, and has been part of you for so long that you don't listen to it anymore. It has become just background noise in your consciousness.

"Nietzsche lost contact with that knowing. To put

it poetically, he stopped listening with his heart and tried to resolve everything with just his mind."

I interjected, "What's wrong with rationality? Shouldn't we put emotions aside?"

He held up his hands, palms toward me, indicating that I should wait, he hadn't finished his thought.

"To answer the really big questions we must rely upon all ways of knowing. You can know things with your mind. That's the most common way of knowing. But you can also know things with your body. Have you ever had the hair on the back of your neck stand up, or felt a shiver run down your spine?"

I nodded. Of course I have, everyone has.

He continued, "That's your body's way of knowing, and quite often it knows things before your brain. You also know things intuitively."

He raised his cup but didn't drink yet.

"We're related to the animals. Geese fly south in the fall, not because they rationalized that winter is coming and they are going to freeze if they stay. They know in a different way to flock together and follow the same flight path every year. A baby knows intuitively that when a nipple is placed in its mouth for the first time, it should suck. You've been in situations where you just knew something wasn't quite right and got yourself the hell out of there before the shit came down."

"Yeah, but is that intuition or is that the subconscious?"

"If it's subconscious," he answered, "knowing without knowing, or knowing without being aware that you know, can we really call it rational? If it's really your brain doing things, calculating, running a subprogram hidden from you, where is that taking place? Where in the mind does that happen? Which neurons are firing? And why is it able to do those calculations so much faster than the conscious mind?"

I didn't have an answer.

"I'm suggesting that the subconscious mind and intuition are either the same thing or they're closely related. Either way they're not rational. They're simply other ways of knowing." He tasted his coffee.

"So what's this have to do with Nietzsche's being afraid of death?"

"So..." He put down his cup. "Nietzsche was no different from anyone else. He knew things he couldn't explain, things that scared him. He knew, like everyone knows, that he was going to die and that the worms were going to eat him. But he refused to ever talk directly about that; he refused to allow himself to even think about that, because if he did, if he accepted the inevitability of it—that he was going to grow old, become weak, slowly lose his sight and his hearing, become impotent, wrinkle, and lose his teeth—then, rationally, his life was meaningless. The only way he could put meaning into his life rationally was to deny the inner voice, to either simply not listen to it or say that it didn't exist.

"That inner voice, that intuition or subconscious or whatever else you want to call it, that thing that tells you that you are destined for greatness—that's your soul whispering in your ear. It's telling you to sit up and pay attention. It's telling you, you don't have much time left, get on with it."

"Get on with what?"

"Get on with living. That's what you're here to do."

"So you don't think Nietzsche was living as fully as he could."

"No, that's not what I am saying. I'm saying he denied his inner voice. If he had listened to it, paid attention to what it was telling him, tried to find where that voice came from, he would have to conclude that it came from nature, or super-nature, or spirit—and he wouldn't have been able to deny God.

"Here's the difference. Nietzsche, and I don't remember if it's in there"—he pointed at the book on the arm of the couch beside me—"or if it's in his other works, argues that man evolved from monkeys. If we evolved from monkeys, then man is just another animal with a bigger brain. There is no inner voice to listen to, and morality becomes something we made up so that we wouldn't exterminate ourselves, rather than something we were born knowing. If we learned our morality, then we came from monkeys. But if we are born knowing right from wrong, then we came from the stars. We either evolved here, came from chance collisions between molecules in a primordial soup and spontaneously became alive, or our origin is much grander than that."

"But if we came from the stars, we had to originate somewhere." I knew that we were getting off-topic, straying from the original thought. I simply needed to challenge him on some point, or I would have to sit passively and be lectured to.

"Origins..." He leaned a little forward. "I showed you time is not linear. Remember time waves?"

I did.

"There is no beginning and end," he continued. "There doesn't have to be a specific point where life began. It could just as well be eternal. If life is a product of the universe and the universe is truly infinite, then we are chasing a rabbit down its hole and entering a world of absurdity when we insist upon only one way of knowing, that being the sterile rational and the denial of all other knowledge."

He stopped. Looked down for a full second, his coffee forgotten on the table beside him.

"It's about that message." He started again, his voice softer. "You know that you were destined for greatness. It's written in your DNA, it's your soul whispering to you, it's your intuition, or your subconscious, it's everywhere except in your rational mind. But you are not alone with that; everyone has it. Some people interpret it to mean that they should go to war and become heroes; some think it means that they should accumulate all the wealth and power that they can; some use it as an excuse to subjugate others. We have a rational mind and an internal message. Our task is to use both, keeping it clear that we are going to die, so wealth and military power and all those other immediate measures of self-worth are inadequate. Greatness must be greatness of spirit, and since all people have the message, it must mean the greatness of humanity and not of the individual. For humanity to become great and achieve its potential, we must individually become great and continue to strive against barbarism; we must seek the end of war, the end of inequality, the end of useless suffering.

"You were born knowing that you were destined for greatness. Everyone is born with that same message written in their DNA. It's what kept the Indians walking on the Trail of Tears. It's what has kept us going despite everything. That kid you see on television with the extended belly and the flies crawling all over him, and they're trying to get you to send money to save him—he has the same message. That's why he stays sitting up, why he doesn't just lie down and die. It's an irrational sense of purpose. Most people have it educated out of them, or, like the kid on television, blocked by trauma, but we all have it. We just have to learn to listen to it again."

I SIT UP under the tree, pull myself from the comfort of the hollow between the roots, and look up at the sky, at the stars, at those pinpoints of distant light, light that travelled for millions of years so that I could look up tonight and see it, and I wonder where he might be in this moment and whether he has a new understanding of his own greatness.

TIME HEALS ALL WOUNDS

THE NEXT SOUND I hear is the buzz of mosquitoes. There's a bit of light in the northeast, a little before sunrise, five-thirty, maybe six. Now I wish I had put up my tent with the screen mesh to keep out the bugs. I lie still for a while, eyes closed, sleeping bag over my head, but it's too hot and stuffy and I'm not going to get back to sleep in any event; may as well get up.

A fire.

A handful of red pine needles — they burn as if they were made out of gasoline — gets it started, a few bigger twigs to keep it going. And once it's flaming nicely, some moss to make smoke to chase the mosquitoes away. I stand in the thick of it and let it

cover me until I smell like burned peat, a more natural insect repellent.

Coffee first, while the fire has a good blaze. It boils
quickly.

Then bacon in a cast-iron frying pan. The fire
is still too hot even for bacon, and I take it off the
flames. The residual heat in the cast iron is sufficient
to brown the half-dozen slices bouncing in their own
grease.

Then, when the fire has died down some, sliced
potatoes until they're beginning to brown before I
add a handful of chopped mushrooms and onion to
complete the fancy hash browns.

And finally, when only coals remain and the frying pan has been scraped clean again, three large eggs
that slowly turn white before I cover them with a lid
and wait patiently, sipping on hot, strong, black coffee.

A good breakfast to start a new day. The eggs are
a little crispy around the edges, but the bacon turned
out perfectly, nicely browned, and the potatoes and
onions and mushrooms have a nice smoky flavour.
Bread toasted on a stick and a couple of thick slices of
cheddar, just to give it a bit more substance.

While I eat, sitting cross-legged on the ground
with the plate on my lap, my coffee cup beside me,

the early light of the new day in the tops of the pine, I begin thinking about time. Is it really the way Clifford told me? Or did he just make all that stuff up? Gravity, black holes, space waves, and whirlpools.

Time.

He'd said time travel was impossible, you can't go forward and backward through it. But he could change the rate of time, speed it up or slow it down. It was, after all, only another wave like space, and if one could be modified, so could the other.

I sip my coffee. Let the thought continue uninterrupted.

Time waves bounce off the surface of the earth and cancel each other out, so time runs slower closer to the surface than higher up. We know this because global positioning systems, GPS, must calculate the time difference between the satellite and the earth, or else the position it gave would be off by several yards.

So maybe he was on to something.

People in emergency situations sometimes describe their experience as though it happened in slow motion. Clifford said that was because they slowed down their personal time. They were still reacting at their normal speed and, to them, it seemed like everyone else was going slower.

So, if he could, like he said, control time…

Why didn't he?

He could have slowed down time and the truck coming across the line would have appeared to be moving in slow motion. He could have gotten out of the way.

Unless…

More probable. He had his time set faster.

"If I need more time, I adjust it so that it runs faster. To everyone around me, it seems like I am moving real slow. It comes in handy when I need extra sleep. I speed up time before I go to bed. I get a full eight or nine hours of sleep, but to the rest of the world only three hours have gone by."

Is that what he was doing? He had a long drive. He'd spent all day packing everything he owned into his truck. He would have been exhausted before he left. Did he speed up his personal time so that the trip wouldn't take as long?

Is that what happened?

Did the drunk guy going north at one time meet Clifford going south at another time, and one or the other miscalculated the time and speed of the other?

Or was it simply that his truck was so overloaded

that he couldn't get out of the way? They had cleaned up the crash site, hauled his truck away to the salvage yard, and brought everything he had to my house. He'd taken pride in his ability to pack. He could fit more things into a truck box than anyone else. The secret, he said, was garbage bags. They fit together without air spaces between. Whatever method he used, the clean-up people needed a three-ton truck to carry everything he had packed in the back of his half-ton.

They came and unceremoniously raised the hoist and dumped it all in my driveway. There was no reason to be careful. It was all broken and rain damaged, and there was very little left for me to salvage. Smashed televisions, the oscilloscope, meters, wires, and transistors, and clothes and books and papers all wet and stuck together.

Maybe when I was packing it all up to take to the garbage dump, I didn't recognize it. What would a time machine look like, anyway?

Maybe that was best. Like he said, the world wasn't ready for it. It would cause too much trouble. Imagine if an Olympic runner had access. They could cheat by adjusting their own time slower so that they raced against people who were in slow motion. Or even worse, if a government got a hold of it and put it on one of their missiles. The country being attacked might not have time to react.

Once the dishes are done and packed away, and my gear stowed, I dig out one of the hardcover notebooks I've brought along. A new page and a new pen; the pen feels good in my hand, comfortable between my fingers. The page is clean and I can smell the paper. I'm back under the pine tree, my back against it. Something draws me here. I don't have to analyze it. It simply feels right.

I put the pen to the paper and begin:

The chair stands on three legs, the fourth broken off and missing. It defies logic, defies gravity. I wonder whether it was the chair. Is that the one? It had once been a pale shade of green that was common in the fifties. Now most of the paint is gone and the wood has turned grey with age.

Is that the one he sat in?

The words come in a purge, a pour of ink onto the page that feels almost like plagiarism. I am a fiction writer, and fiction writers create their stories with will and determination; we wrestle the text into existence. Writing memoir feels like I am stealing, simply recounting memories.

I review: *The chair stands on three legs,* a metaphor for Clifford, Dad, and Mom. Wonder if I should work that into the manuscript or leave it for the reader to figure out? I leave it for the reader.

Ink and paper, and place, and pine tree combine into cathartic pleasure, and before I stop for another coffee, pull the pot from the still-hot ashes, I have written over a thousand words.

I am okay. I might not be healed, but I have felt the beginning of healing.

I will go to the cemetery where we buried him yesterday, where the sand is still fresh from our digging. I will stand beside that mound covered in flowers, some still fresh, others made of plastic, and I will leave his hula hoop with him, his bubble maker, and imagine my brother travelling among the stars.

ACKNOWLEDGEMENTS

My sincerest thanks to Gregory Lyndon, who read the earliest draft and suggested necessary changes. To Stephanie Sinclair for her suggestions with the original manuscript. To Janie Yoon for her incredible insight. To Patricia Sanders for her keen eye. And to my wife, Joan, who became nearly as emotionally attached to the work as I am.

Photo: Calvin Fehr

HAROLD R. JOHNSON is the author of five works of fiction and two works of nonfiction. His previous book, *Firewater: How Alcohol Is Killing My People (and Yours)*, was a finalist for the Governor General's Literary Award for Nonfiction. Born and raised in northern Saskatchewan to a Swedish father and a Cree mother, he is a graduate of Harvard Law School and managed a private practice for several years before becoming a Crown prosecutor. Johnson is a member of the Montreal Lake Cree Nation and lives at the north end of Montreal Lake, Saskatchewan, with his wife, Joan.